The Teenage Guide to
Friends

**To everyone who wants to see into the minds
of the people around them.**

All the advice in this book is given in good faith and after a great deal
of care and consideration. However, every situation is different
and sometimes effective and safe advice requires specific knowledge
of that situation. If you have any doubts or if your situation seems
different from those described here, please always seek help
from a trusted adult such as a teacher, professional or other
person who cares about you.

First published 2017 by Walker Books Ltd
87 Vauxhall Walk, London SE11 5HJ

2 4 6 8 10 9 7 5 3 1

Text © 2017 Nicola Morgan

The right of Nicola Morgan to be identified as author and illustrator respectively
of this work has been asserted by them in accordance with the Copyright, Designs
and Patents Act 1988

This book has been typeset in Clarendon and Shinn

Printed in Great Britain by Clays Ltd, St Ives plc

British Library Cataloguing in Publication Data:
a catalogue record for this book is available from the British Library

ISBN: 978-1-4063-6977-9

www.walker.co.uk

NICOLA MORGAN

The Teenage Guide to Friends

with a foreword by
Cathy Cassidy

WALKER BOOKS
AND SUBSIDIARIES

LONDON • BOSTON • SYDNEY • AUCKLAND

Contents

SECTION ONE

SECTION TWO

SECTION THREE

Foreword

I wish I'd had this book when I was growing up…
A book to tell me that it was OK to be shy, that it
was fine not to be "in with the in-crowd", that it
was normal to have problems and fall-outs. There
are a million and one things that can derail a
teenage friendship – especially now, when the extra
challenge of social media can feel relentless. Yet
this is a point in our lives when friends matter more
than ever before. When things unravel, it can feel
like the end of the world.

So how do you steer your way through and learn
to build healthy, happy, lasting friendships? How
do you even begin to understand why people do the
things they do when you can't always work out why
you have acted a certain way? Trust me, it can
take a very long time to learn it all by trial and
error, and that's where this awesome book comes in.
Honest, open, practical and positive, it offers a clear,
easy-to-understand guide to why friendships matter,
how they can go wrong and, more importantly, how
they can go right.

In the twelve years I spent as agony aunt for *Shout*
magazine, friendship issues were the number-one
problem young people were struggling with. Now, as
a novelist for teens and pre-teens, I probably get

more "problem page" types of questions from my readers than I ever did when I was an official agony aunt. Friendship is at the heart of all my books, and fiction is a great way to understand ourselves and others, but occasionally we need something more. I've learned a lot from this book, and I think every teenager should have a copy ... because friendship matters.

Cathy Cassidy

Introduction

Whether our friendships are going well or not makes a massive difference to our happiness and wellbeing. This is true whatever age we are. I don't think anyone can go through life without some stressful times with friends – or enemies, or people who are supposed to be friends but behave more like enemies. While you're at school, it can be much harder. It's a very intense time and you're surrounded by so many people every day, all with different personalities, needs and behaviours. Some of those people are positive influences and some are not. Often, peer group and friendship situations are really painful. You'll wonder how someone could be so mean, cruel, careless or selfish.

Thing is, humans are complex creatures who don't always behave in sensible and positive ways. We're emotional and often not very well controlled. We say the wrong things, do the wrong things. We fail to understand each other. Adults do all that, too.

But this book is about much more than solving problems! In a way, it's a book about empathy – the ability to understand what someone else is feeling – and human psychology. It tries to get inside the heads of the people around you to see how they might be feeling and thinking – because how they are thinking and feeling affects how they behave towards you. We can't be sure exactly what someone else is feeling, but the more we try to understand them, the closer we will come. And the better we understand other people's behaviour, the better we can manage our relationships and not beat ourselves up when someone behaves in a cruel or thoughtless way.

So, if you're interested in the fascinating ways that differences in personality or life experiences affect our behaviour, read on! You'll find clear explanations, advice, strategies and things to think about. Some of the advice or situations won't apply to you: ignore those and focus on what you feel does apply to you and will help you. Everyone is different and *The Teenage Guide to Friends* tries to celebrate that as well as understand it. At the end of the book, there's a list of resources for all the topics I cover.

MY SHORT PERSONAL STORY

My own childhood was one of not fitting in. During my primary school years, my sister and I were the only girls in a boys' school because my parents taught there and there wasn't anywhere else we could go. And in my secondary school, I was much younger than everyone in my year. I was eleven when I started at that school and the others were nearly thirteen. An eleven-year-old girl who has only ever played with boys is very different from a teenage girl, believe me!

I felt more different than when I'd been at the boys'

school. I didn't know about any of the things the girls seemed so expert and interested in. I was geeky, swotty, skinny, undeveloped. They seemed to speak a different language from me. They thought I was the clever one in the class; I thought I was the boring one that no one wanted to hang out with. I wasn't bullied but I was left out. At weekends, my main aim was to find out what everyone else was doing, so I could tag along. If I didn't, I'd be left behind and no one would notice I wasn't there. They weren't mean about it; I was just invisible.

So, if you feel you don't fit in for any reason, I understand.

Did it damage me, wreck my life, stop me making great friendships later? No. Not in the slightest. I just learnt a bit late. Actually, I think it makes me a better person because I'm now very sensitive to people being left out.

A NOTE ABOUT THE QUIZZES

The personality quizzes in this book are informal and have not been scientifically tested. They are just the start of finding out more about yourself and to give you some extra insight.

Whatever answers you come up with, don't make the mistake of saying, "Right, that's how I am and there's nothing I can do to change it." If we discover that our personality makes us behave in a certain way and if we would prefer to behave differently, we can alter our behaviour and thinking and so improve our lives. But remember that you will naturally change as you grow older, so don't get too hung up on your personality type: it doesn't define you.

Besides, people don't fit neatly into boxes and it isn't helpful to try to fit yourself into one or label yourself. These personality tests give us clues and explanations about our behaviour, that's all. We are all different and it's interesting to understand the differences.

I suggest you don't write your answers on the pages of this book: I think it's better if you keep them to yourself. Although it's fun to do the tests with a friend – and of course you can do that if you want to – it's also likely that you'll be more honest if you do them privately.

TRUSTED ADULTS

You don't have to deal with problems on your own. Talk to an adult you trust if you would like to. That might be your parents or carers, a teacher at school, or another adult. It could be someone at Childline, especially if the problem feels as though it is damaging your life and you don't know how to deal with it (see Resources).

On friendship issues, it usually makes sense to talk to someone who knows you and, perhaps, who knows the others involved. That person might have more relevant suggestions than a stranger. So, one of your teachers would often be a good start. Your school should make it clear who you can go to with problems, but you can also speak to a different teacher if there's one you feel more comfortable talking to.

However, I realize that sometimes adults don't help when it comes to friendship issues! Adults might regard something as a trivial reason to be upset. For example, if someone is giving you the silent treatment, adults may not realize just how horrible this feels. Or if there's been an argument or a problem, they might say things like, "Oh, it'll all be fine," or "Just shake hands and everything will be sorted." Although that advice might be right in the end, the problem is that you feel much worse than the adult realizes.

It can also be difficult asking adults because you might believe you're going to be judged. I can't promise adults won't judge you, of course, but I think the trick is how you approach the question. If you start by saying, "I know you might think this is silly, but I need you to know that it's really upsetting me," you have a good chance of getting a sympathetic response.

Whatever your doubts or fears, it's still important to know that you can ask for help, especially if there's a situation you think is either getting worse or is frightening.

SECTION ONE

What Are Friends?

Different types of animals behave in different ways. One difference is whether they tend to live in structured groups, alone or in pairs – how "social" they generally are. Some species almost always live in groups or packs and are described as being more social. Think of dogs compared with cats. Cats act more independently and seem "happier" on their own. Of course, they can form friendships when they happen to live together, but they don't naturally stay in close groups. Dogs are usually different: when dogs are kept as pets they treat their family as their "pack" and seem to need company. They may even become ill if they are too isolated.

Humans have extremely large, complicated social networks, beginning with their immediate family and spreading more widely to relatives, groups of friends and other contacts. This was true even before social media came along to create far bigger networks.

Social behaviours have been built into our biology

over thousands of years of evolution. However, one of the special things about humans is how individual we all are. Different dogs behave differently, depending on things like their breed and how they were reared. But humans, being incredibly complex, have far more individual differences.

Also, because of our powerful brains and ability to think rationally and use self-control, we can often make choices that push against those thousands of years of evolution. For example, although human adults in most societies tend to form a tight "pair bond", many choose not to. We have that power. Humans, like all animal species, are evolved to reproduce and pass on their genes, yet many people opt not to. So, we don't have to be dominated by everything evolution makes other animals do. We have some choices.

One other aspect of being human is that we have created lots of ways of supporting each other, through various sorts of friendships. Using empathy, we can understand, value and respect different bonds and lifestyles, including very social and more solitary ones. In fact, it's partly empathy that allows us to have large social groups in the first place. Scientists have argued that the bigger the brain a species has, the larger the possible network of "friends". (I'll talk more about that later.)

Because we are each unique and have some control over our behaviour, in theory we can choose the sort

16

of social life we feel comfortable with. For some people, this means having a wide circle of friends and for others it means enjoying the close friendship of a small number. Finding your own way through these choices can be very difficult during adolescence, because you are changing all the time and so are the people around you. You may feel pushed towards friendships that don't actually suit you. Also, you have fewer choices than adults about who to spend time with. You usually have very little control over which school you go to; or, if you're home-schooled, your choices are limited by where you live and what is available to you.

SOCIAL SUPPORT

The point of friends is support. That's why it can feel so bad when friendships go wrong. But you have more than friends: you have social groups, too. Your social groups consist of people you've had some kind of contact with: it could be your friend, brother, teacher, neighbour, aunt, employer, postman, doctor, step-cousin, etc. Some are close to you; others are not. Some you might only have contact with once a year or less; others you see every day. Even if you think you don't have that many friends, you do have people who will support you.

We need these groups. The world is a scary place and we sometimes need help with the choices we make. We can achieve far more if we work together, supporting each other. Then, when we're ill, old, injured, tired, confused or all sorts of other things, our groups are there for us. We need to know who to rely on, and if we've picked the right people they will be happy to help us.

Because human social systems are so complicated, it can take a long time to learn how they work. When you're a young child, it's much simpler because your group is really small – usually your parents, or one parent or carer, and maybe a brother or sister (or more!). Then you probably go to nursery and learn to get on with a few other small children and some adults you haven't met before. Primary school is a bit more complicated: you spend most of the time with your classmates and a few adults. The adults can usually keep an eye on things and make sure that you're coping with friendships and that everyone is treating each other well. (Ideally.) During that time, you discover that you like some people and not others. You learn that people behave differently and some make you feel good and others don't. You learn what happens if you smile, hug, cry, borrow a pencil without asking, or hit someone.

Secondary school adds a whole extra layer of complication: bigger classes, different classes for different subjects, more teachers, teams, groups, clubs. It's much harder for adults to spot problems. And you're all changing, too, becoming teenagers and then moving towards being adults.

To sum up, humans are, by nature, social animals, but there are two things that make us different from other animals: first, we have unusually large and complicated social systems, which can be difficult to negotiate and fit into. Second, our powerful brains give us choices, including the possibility of being different from the people around us if we wish. But that is a difficult choice, and mostly we spend our time and energy trying to find the right social groups that can support our needs and where we feel comfortable and useful. We need to be useful, because if we are useful to our group, it will look after us.

Group behaviour can cause problems, too, as I'll talk about later. But for now, the important thing is that humans need these connections. Some only need a small group – the number of friends you have is not a sign of your success at being human. Others thrive in big groups. It's important to value each type of person equally and not to worry if you don't have masses of friends. What matters is that they give you what you need and you give them what they need. That's how friendship works: it's a two-way thing.

WHAT IS A FRIEND?

One thing's for sure: friends are not what certain social media platforms would have you think. Those are mostly just contacts and most of them are not, in my opinion, friends. Here's what I think a "friend" is: someone you know and like enough to be happy to spend time with. You believe they feel similarly towards you. They would want to help you if you had a problem, and you would help them. They would not let you sit on your own at lunch. You know enough about them to feel that you trust each other to some extent. You feel fairly comfortable around them and they share many of your beliefs, values, likes and dislikes. Most of the time, you understand the person, as though you are "on the same wavelength".

This doesn't mean you have to like and dislike all the same things or agree about everything; and you don't have to reveal everything about yourself or trust all your friends with your deepest secrets. But there are enough positive bonds between you for you both to feel a proper human connection. Perhaps your heart lifts a little when you see the person. Imagine you bumped into them on holiday: you'd be happy and you'd want to stop for a chat.

Your friendship might change over time. That's OK. You're human: you change. Don't be afraid of that.

HOW MANY FRIENDS DO YOU NEED?

You might feel you don't have enough friends. But who says what "enough" is? How many will you think is enough? Remember I said that some people like to have lots of friends and others prefer a few? Let's look at that more closely. It's not as simple as it seems.

You see that really "popular" or cool girl who seems to have loads of friends? She looks relaxed and confident and people just seem to gravitate towards her. In a group, she's the centre of attention and you can't imagine her ever being left out of anything that's going on. Or what about that boy who always seems to be the life and soul of the party? You can't imagine him being bullied or ignored or anyone being mean to him. No one would dare, you think.

Hang on. You're assuming they are happy and that they have a strong support network of friends. You might be right but you might be wrong. The fact that they're relaxed in company and don't seem as self-conscious as you feel doesn't tell you anything about their happiness or inner confidence. They might be one of those extrovert personalities who tend not to be so self-conscious. Or they may have grown up in a big family with loads of chances to practise social interaction. Or they may be quite insensitive and not care much about what people think. So, yes, social situations may look easy for them, but that doesn't necessarily mean that they have perfect friendships.

They might crave a close and trusting friendship which they don't get from their "fans". Perhaps they're dealing with complicated groupings and break-ups among their friends. Maybe they have high-maintenance friendships or their popularity exposes them to jealousy. Or perhaps they have shallow friendships, after which their so-called friends move on, leaving those popular-looking people behind. You really can't tell.

And don't assume that people who seem to have lots of friends have better or easier friendships than others.

You see those students who often keep to themselves during break or lunch and don't join in noisy chatter or games, preferring quieter activities they can do on their own? You might be assuming they're unhappy and don't have a good support network of friends. You could be right but you could be wrong. Perhaps they have a couple of really close friends, people they can privately trust and who can trust them. They might like being on their own some of the time. They might be strong "introverts" (see **Introvert or Extrovert?** in SECTION FOUR) and they might need quiet time to think, dream, be creative or just wind down. Introverts may not be the life and soul of the party, but they can be very happy and have wonderful friendships.

Remember again: not everyone needs lots of friends. And not everyone shows their friendship with linked arms and hugs. Although everyone needs some contacts and connections, we don't all need them all the time. We don't all need our friendships to be out there.

So, my answer to the question "How many friends do you need?" is: enough to feel supported, enough that we know we've got someone to go to and that we can feel useful to them when they need it. That could be one person or thirty. You're not a better person if you have thirty friends. Don't spend time worrying about whether you have enough friends; just get involved in activities you enjoy and friends will come. (But you will find tips for making more friends in SECTION TWO.)

DO BOYS AND GIRLS
DO FRIENDSHIP DIFFERENTLY?

This is a really complicated question! Lots of people talk about differences but these differences may be exaggerated. It's too easy to fall back on stereotypes of how different genders behave. Whether we were brought up to be a boy or a girl, and what sort of boy or girl, can make such a difference to our behaviours. Maybe if children were all brought up exactly the same, regardless of gender, they would behave the same in their friendships. We can't really know. What we can know is "how things often are". The world we have to deal with is the one we have, not the ideal one.

Here's what I think: you don't have to conform to anyone else's needs or behaviours. Whether you like friendships where you can discuss your innermost feelings, or you want to keep your feelings hidden, or you want whatever types of friendship suit you, the choice is yours. Don't be trapped by stereotypes. Do what makes you feel comfortable and look for friends who are

23

understanding and accepting of who you are.

If you find that difficult at school, because you don't have a choice of who's around you, see if you can make friends outside school – in local activities, for example. And look ahead to the time when you'll leave school and be able to have more control over friendship groups.

CAN BOYS AND GIRLS BE "JUST GOOD FRIENDS"?

Of course! Because people become friends with each other when they share opinions, values and tastes, and you can share those with people of any gender.

In secondary school, hormones are kicking in and you might be physically attracted to someone in much more than a "just good friends" way. But if you're not physically attracted to someone and you like each other, you can certainly be good friends regardless of gender.

There can be complications, mainly because of other people's perceptions. Ignore them. If you feel safe and comfortable and both of you want the same thing from your friendship, ignore everyone else.

One thing to remember, though: if you have a good friend who is a different gender from you, they may also want to hang out with friends of the same gender sometimes. You need to accept that.

Different friendships bring different benefits. Celebrate them all.

CAN YOU BE FRIENDS WITH SOMEONE MUCH YOUNGER OR OLDER?

A friendship with someone much younger or older than you is not an equal friendship. You may both get something out of it but the older person is almost certainly "dominant" over the younger. This makes it something to be cautious about.

First, it depends on how big the gap is. It's usual for friendships to be within the same year group and some-times schools discourage friendships that cross year groups. Being friends with someone just one year above or below might not seem that big a deal – and usually wouldn't be a problem outside – but it can lead to problems in school environments and that's what the school may want to avoid. Mainly, the problems are minor or unpredictable: teasing for one or both of you; disruption of the peer groups surrounding you; or the fact that you both might be less involved in the activities for your specific year group, leading to isolation for either or both of you and, if the friendship breaks down, even more trouble for you.

The larger the age gap, the greater the potential problems and the more likely adults are to discourage the friendship. If the age gap is more than one school year group, there would be concerns about the younger one "growing up too fast" or being involved in activities that aren't appropriate for that age, such as going to parties with older teenagers or becoming sexually active. You

25

might feel you want to grow up fast, but there's no long-term advantage to that. However, you might feel that you are more mature than your year group and be naturally drawn to older teenagers. Or you might be old for your year and closer in age to students in the year above. This is very understandable.

But be aware of possible difficulties. Remember that you are both changing and you are likely to be changing at different rates. If your friend is much older, they will leave school long before you and soon be in the world of work. It's likely that your friendship will become more difficult, especially once they've left school, so it's really important that you keep strong links with the other students in your year group, otherwise you could feel isolated.

If your friend is much younger, perhaps you get a sense of status from having their peer group look up to you. I understand this but I don't think it's very healthy for your own growth if you rely on it. It's great that you're giving support to a younger teenager but this is a different sort of friendship from the ones we have with our peers. As an adult, your peers will naturally include people of different ages but in adolescence that's much harder.

When we're young, a few years makes a lot of difference. Think how different an eleven-year-old is from a thirteen-year-old – just two to three years but a huge leap in development, desires, outlook, behaviours and emotions. Of course, some people are more mature than others at the same age, and so age difference can seem less in some people than in others, but I still don't think you'll find many eleven-year-olds whose minds work in the same way as that of a thirteen- or fourteen-year-old.

As you get older, age differences matter less and less. A twenty-five-year-old and a thirty-year-old can be indistinguishable, and once you're into your thirties even more differences have melted away.

So, the best friendships during teenage years are usually between people of roughly the same age, and friendships between teenagers who are two or more school years apart are potentially difficult. I'm not saying don't be friends: just make sure that it is a two-way friendship and that you have friends of your own age as well.

ARE ADULTS YOUR FRIENDS?

What if there's an adult you consider as your friend? I think we need to be clear what we mean by "friend". Supposing your home situation means you don't have good and consistent support from your parents or other carers; or you only have one parent and that parent is not the same gender as you, so you rely on the support and friendship of an adult of your gender. (Many people don't find gender relevant but others do. Only you know whether this is important to you.) In those cases, the friendship of another adult can be incredibly helpful. But I think you'd agree that this relationship is more like one you could have with a trusted older relative than with someone your age. It's very different from the sort of friendship I'm talking about in this book.

Ask yourself these questions about your adult friend:

- Do they encourage me to have lots of other friends?
- Do I always feel comfortable with this person?
- Does someone I trust think I spend too much time with this person?

If your answers were Yes, Yes and No, this sounds like a healthy relationship and it is, by most definitions, a friendship.

If not, it's wrong for me to make judgements without knowing the circumstances but I believe you should think carefully about whether this friendship is benefiting you. A person who prevents you from having other friends is not a proper friend. You need to feel comfortable and safe. Why does someone else think you spend too much time with them? (They may be wrong or right.) Is it possible that you're allowing yourself to be over-protected? In any case, if you're in doubt, do talk to somebody you trust.

Even a positive friendship with an adult is not enough to provide the bonds and connections you need as you move towards adulthood. If you really trust this adult, one of the best things they could do for you is help you find ways of also making friends your own age.

I hope you have adults in your life who support you and who you like being with. But I hope you also see that the relationships you have with them are different from the equal friendships you can have with people your age.

THINGS TO THINK ABOUT

- Remember that you really only know about one person's experience: your own. You can guess what other people feel about their friendships, but you can be sure that many people who seem confident and popular also have problems and heartache.
- Can you remember when you first met one of your current friends? Did you know immediately that you would be friends? What did you first notice about them? Who spoke first?
- Some people say "opposites attract", meaning that people are often friends with someone who is very different to them. Do you agree with this? Think about some of the ways you're different from any of your friends. Does it matter?

What is important in a friend? Put the following in order of importance:
- They laugh a lot – and about the same things as me.

- They would never laugh at me.
- I can trust them with a secret.
- I believe they feel the same way about me as I do about them.
- I feel equal to them in most ways.
- They will help me when I'm feeling down.
- If they have to tell me something I don't want to hear, they will do it sensitively and kindly.

Not all your friends need to have the same positive features but they should all give you some good feelings most of the time.

Negative friendships

Not all friendships are positive or healthy and it's important to know the signs of those that aren't.

ONE-WAY FRIENDSHIPS

Good friendships are "two-way", not "one-way". A one-way friendship is where one person gives everything and gets nothing. Some people love "giving", so they might be very happy looking after the other person all the time. Generosity makes the giver feel good, too, so that person might seem quite happy about it.

Even so, we need to be careful about such one-sided friendships. Although the giver might be genuinely happy to do all the giving, the person receiving the care and attention may soon feel inadequate because they can't give back. That's why this can be a fragile sort of friendship and may not last in the long term.

If you're in a friendship where you're doing all the giving, are you OK with this? And do you think your friend is happy? Of course, if a person is going through a really bad patch, they do need help and may not be able to give help back. But at some point, either the person receiving the help is likely to feel bad about not being able to repay this kindness, or the person giving all the help is going to need something in return. It may be possible to have a long-term unequal friendship, but only if both sides are

100% happy with their role and I question whether that's likely. Good friendships, the ones that last a long time, usually need equality. The self-esteem of both people depends on it.

In any friendship, there'll be times when one person needs more help and support than the other. And good two-way friendships handle this well. The person needing support knows that last month they gave support, so feels OK to accept it. Both friends feel equally valuable and both get a buzz out of helping each other when one of them is in need. And, really, this is what friendship is: a partnership, to support each other. Good friendship is about enjoying the good times and supporting each other through bad times. That's why friendship is so important.

FRENEMIES, FAKE FRIENDS
AND TOXIC FRIENDSHIPS

Some friendships can be negative for one of the friends. This is not the same as "one-way" friendship, where one person needs all the support. Negative friendships are more complicated and there are many different sorts and different reasons for them. We sometimes call these "toxic" because they have a poisoning effect on the friendship, with one side suffering pain and damage to their wellbeing and self-esteem.

Here are some signs of a toxic relationship:

- The other person always seems to be in control; you feel manipulated.
- You never quite know whether it's going to be a good day or a bad day for your friendship.
- Your friend behaves very differently when other people are around, perhaps ignoring you or being mean to you in front of other people.
- Your friend hates it when you spend time with anyone else, making you feel uncomfortable or making you feel you need to hide the fact.
- You don't feel comfortable around this person and you feel as if you have to change who you are.
- Your friend often makes you feel bad about yourself, saying nasty, undermining or critical things, whether accidentally or on purpose, such as little comments about your body, hair, face.
- Your friend needs constant praise for his/her talents/looks, etc. and never praises you back.
- When you try to explain how you feel, your friend laughs at you and you can't seem to make them understand.
- Your friend asks you to do something that makes you uncomfortable. You feel that you should do it to prove your friendship.
- You feel you have to work really hard to gain

your friend's respect and that they are always judging you.

• You know they behave badly but you think you can change them.

No one is perfect. So you can forgive your friend some bad behaviour. Later I'll be explaining some of the reasons why people sometimes behave badly. But, if it goes on too long and is making you feel bad about yourself, consider whether this is really friendship. Friendship is supposed to make people feel good! Enemies are people who make you feel bad. This is why we call this sort of person a "frenemy": someone you think of as a friend but who behaves like an enemy.

Frenemies can wreck your sense of worth. You might allow such a friendship to continue because you don't think you're worth more than that. You are worth more: walk away. There are better people out there to be friends with.

THINGS TO THINK ABOUT

• When you were reading about negative friendships, did you find yourself thinking of someone who is making your life tough at the moment? Has it helped you feel better about it or made you see that it isn't your fault?

• If you think about your various friendships, you

might start to compare them with each other. I don't think it's necessary or helpful to do this. Not all friendships have to be brilliant all the time. A friendship that's not going too well for you now or is causing you upset could change and become a really valuable one later.

Online friendships – social media

The rise of social media is incredibly recent. It wasn't around when your parents were your age. It has allowed us all to be in contact with huge numbers of people from many different backgrounds and cultures. When your parents were teenagers, they could really only meet people who lived near them.

Those of us who use social media would describe many people as friends who we haven't met in real life. But are they friends? All of them? Does it matter if they are different types of friends from the face-to-face sort that we've had for thousands of years? I believe there are some things to be cautious about as well as the many advantages to celebrate. And there are strategies to help us negotiate possible problems. Since your parents didn't have to deal with this, they need to learn them, too.

CAN YOU HAVE REAL FRIENDS ONLINE?

Yes! It's entirely possible to have a really good, strong friendship and never meet the person in real life. That's relatively unusual, however, because if you're really good friends with them, you'll probably want to meet.

We normally benefit from being able to see the other person and physically spend time with them. That allows us to experience using all our senses. Touch is very important to humans, for example. That's why you often see friends touching each other, even pushing, shoving, nudging, and going round with arms linked. Young children naturally want to hold hands with their friends, though by the time you're a teenager, holding hands has come to mean something more specific: in fact, holding hands with a romantic partner is one of the stages in a relationship, a sort of marking that "we are together".

We talk about being "close" to someone or being "close friends" because friends tend to want to be physically closer – and are allowed to be. Being online doesn't enable that.

Also, eye contact and body language are a major part of human communication, giving extra insight into what the other person may be feeling or thinking. The fact that online communication is usually without eye contact is what makes cyber-bullying and online arguments so common. Also, many arguments arise from texts or online messages because one person thought the other was being rude or sarcastic, and all because they couldn't hear their voice or see their face.

Nevertheless, it is possible to have a good friendship that is only online. You have to work at it, though. In fact, you may have to work harder if you're to build the bonds that friendship needs to become strong. But if you enjoy communicating with someone online more than you enjoy actually hanging out with them, that's OK. Sometimes, it's just how it works.

GOOD THINGS ABOUT SOCIAL MEDIA

Making friends online has lots of advantages. You can get to know people from a wide range of backgrounds and cultures, far more than you will usually come across at school. For people in rural communities or small towns, it can be the only way to be in contact with a variety of people. I think making friends with people from different countries and backgrounds is really important, helping us be more understanding and open-minded.

The online world is also great for anyone who finds it difficult to know what to say face to face. On a social media platform or online forum, you can take those first steps without the extra stress of speaking and making eye contact. You can find out a lot about the other person – such as whether you have similar likes and dislikes, interests and opinions. For example, if you'd identified someone you might like to be friends with at school one day but you hadn't had a chance to chat much, an online conversation would be an easy way to develop a friendship. You'd get an idea of their sense of humour, how kind they are, whether they think in the same way as you.

You can also easily find people with particular shared interests. Shared interests are not only a big clue as to who you will get on with but also give you something to talk about straightaway. So, if you like books or films, you'll find online communities of teenagers discussing books or films. Every hobby or sport you can think of will be represented out there in the online world.

If you have a particular difficulty, anxiety or disability, or a personal or family situation that makes you want to talk to others who have been through the same, there will be support groups for people who share your life circumstances and concerns.

Finally, if you feel "different" from the people you happen to be at school with, the online world gives you the chance to find people your age that you can identify with. Isolation becomes less likely for all these reasons.

PROBLEMS WITH SOCIAL MEDIA

There are well-known dangers and disadvantages to online friendships. These possible problems should not make you avoid an incredibly powerful form of communication, but they should definitely make you be careful and wise. If you know the risks, you can more easily avoid them.

So, let's take a look at the dangers of online friendships.

First, since you can't see the person, you could easily be deceived. It could be in a small way – a boy saying he is five feet eight when he is really five feet three. Who cares? Or in a big way – someone claiming to be a fourteen-year-old girl, just like you, when in fact it's a forty-eight-year-old man. You'll have heard frightening stories of people who believed they were communicating with someone their own age, only to discover that they were being lied to and "groomed" by someone with very bad intentions indeed. Any adult pretending to be a teenager and befriending you can only have bad motives. Believe those stories, because they have happened and they will probably happen again. Please make sure they don't happen to you. You might think no one could trick you like that, but victims describe how convincing the other person was and how shocked they were to discover that someone they thought was a friend their own age was nothing of the sort.

Never risk meeting anyone for the first time without taking somebody with you and making sure that the meeting place is safe and public. Take no risks at all with this. I say exactly the same to adults. Anyone of any age can be tricked and badly hurt.

Second, it can happen that a person you get on with really well online turns out to be someone you don't get on with when you meet. They didn't deceive you deliberately so it's not dangerous but it can be disappointing. Thing is, it's often easy to begin a friendship online and harder to maintain it in real life. In online friendships, the "chemistry" isn't there, because it comes from being with a person and getting good vibes from their facial expressions and how they react to you. So, it's easy to get on with someone in written words but then find that the chemistry doesn't happen when you meet. Those friends will probably stay as online friends. That's OK.

Third, if the reason you prefer online friendships is that you find real-life chat difficult or scary, take care not to over-use the Internet as a hiding place. If there's something we find difficult but we will benefit from doing, we need to be brave and face it. We feel good about ourselves when we've overcome a challenge and you already know that social interaction is a human need, even if some people need much less than others. Psychologists say that having enough human contact is important for mental health and wellbeing. So, online friendships are great, and feeling the need to hide sometimes is normal, but it's also important to have face-to-face interaction, and confront the things we find difficult.

If you feel you may be using the online world as too much of a hiding place, try to find ways to build one or two real-world friendships, even if it's hard at first. You will find strategies in this book.

Finally, most people aren't entirely honest online. They select the best or most dramatic pictures or posts about themselves. They "self-censor", only choosing things that show the side they want to reveal. We all, to some extent, act a part, showing the aspects of ourselves that we want to show. We do that face-to-face as well, modifying thoughts and emotions to present a particular picture to the world, but it's easier to do it online and so we may do it more. There are things we don't want other people

41

to know about our thoughts – quite rightly, as those thoughts might be embarrassing or, usually, very boring! This means that what you see online is only a snapshot and might give you the impression that everyone has a more exciting or more perfect life than you.

The rewards of online communication are huge but the rewards of face-to-face contact are biologically important to us and give us a truer picture of other people and the world. A balance of both is probably best.

CAN YOU HAVE TOO MANY FRIENDS?

Yes! And it could be bad for your mental health!

Scientists say that different animal species can "manage" different numbers of friends, depending on their brain size, and that humans can manage larger groups than other species. But there's a limit to this. Evolutionary psychologist Robin Dunbar worked out that, based on human brain size, the most number of "friends" or relationships we can each manage, on average, is 150. This is called "Dunbar's number" (see Resources). He talks about different levels of friendship, with close friendships requiring more contact and management. The point is that all friendships do take time to maintain and there isn't enough time to "look after" more than a certain number of friends. If you've reached the most you can manage and then make new friendships, some of your old ones will naturally fade. For example, when you leave school and go to university or a job, you won't keep up with all your school friends because you'll be spending time with new friends.

What's this got to do with social media? Well, depending on how much time you spend online and how hard you work at your online friendships, you may have, according to your stats, many more than 150. They aren't real friends (though some may be). They include contacts and acquaintances. And you can't actually manage them: you can't properly know, like and spend time with all of them. They don't all care about you and you don't care about all of them. Will they all rush to help you when you need them? Will you rush to help them all when they need you? Be honest!

So, although social networking has allowed us to make lots of friends easily, it has also stretched our networks so widely that we can't maintain them. And trying to can cause stress. Some people make the mistake of thinking it's all about how many friends you have, rather than how good those friends are. It's too much about getting "likes" and affirmation. If you use social media, you know that little heart-lift you get when you see you've got a certain number of likes or favourites on your latest post or picture? That's a little rush of the chemical dopamine – the brain's reward chemical – and it's addictive. You want more and more of it, and your happiness starts to depend on how many people "liked" the photo of you grinning at a funfair. Doesn't sound too great, does it?

So, our online friends can give us something: fun, contact, support, advice. But we need to be a bit wise about these friendships. They are not enough. And there can be too many for our own good.

Consider whether you'd be happier with a few good friends – friends who would really help you when you needed it and who actually care – rather than all those lists of people you've never met and who don't properly care about you.

ONLINE CRUELTY AND CYBER-BULLYING

Unfortunately, being online can make some people behave really badly and be incredibly unkind and thoughtless.

There are several main reasons for this:

- Making comments online is incredibly easy. People can fire off an insult or cruel comment in a couple of seconds and then get straight back to what they're doing. They don't have to go anywhere or make any effort at all. It's as though there are no consequences for them. If they made that same comment to someone's face, they'd have to continue the discussion; online, they can just do it and forget it.

- Being able to be anonymous gives a cruel person or bully extra confidence. They believe they can do things without being caught or punished. (Actually, it's very hard to be truly anonymous and there are many ways for them to be discovered.)

- There is no eye contact or other visual clue to show that the victim of a nasty comment has been affected. So a cruel person can be tempted just to say more and more. Again, no consequences for the nasty person. This is part of what scientists call "the online disinhibition effect" – the fact that people are less inhibited or careful online. It's something we are only now beginning to understand.

- Cruelty and anger are natural human traits – which doesn't mean they are "right". (Actually, often anger is right – for example, if someone treats you badly, it's justifiable to feel angry, although we must learn to control our reaction to that feeling.) I think the Internet allows us to be uncontrolled, because it's so easy to fire off a quick response, and then it's hard to take the comment back. If someone is a spiteful person who gets pleasure from hurting others or has problems with anger management, then the Internet makes it horribly easy for them to act out their cruelty or rage.

- Many people are poor at thinking ahead to the consequences of an action; some people are more impulsive than others, finding it harder to control their instant desire to do something. The part of the brain we need for this – the prefrontal cortex – is the part that finishes developing last, not until well into your twenties. So teenagers often find it harder to look ahead and think, *Hmm, if I do that, X might happen and I don't want that.* Or, even if they work out what might happen, the emotional desire to do something can simply be too strong. (You'll find references to teenage brain development in Resources.)

- Connected to that, there's often "group behaviour" when it comes to Internet bullying or online nastiness. If your group is being unpleasant to someone, it can be hard to stand up and say, "This isn't OK." Sometimes, people go along with online bullying simply because their friends are doing it. I'll talk about this more in the chapter on Peer Pressure and Group Behaviour.

- Finally, although many teenagers are very caring, scientists have discovered that, on average, teenagers (especially younger ones) struggle more than other age groups with empathy – the ability to understand what someone else is feeling. Often, it's not that you can't be empathetic, just that you may be overwhelmed by stress and emotion. Empathy is harder online, because you don't have body language and facial expressions to help. (If you're interested in this research, I have included references for you in Resources.)

THINGS TO THINK ABOUT

- Do you find that social media helps you with your friendships or not?
- Do you have any friends who seem to behave quite differently on social media than in real life?
- Have you ever said anything online that you afterwards wished you hadn't said? Can you use the memory to help you avoid something similar again?
- Have you or your friends had a major problem caused by behaviour online? What did you learn from it?
- "Think before you type and pause before you send" is a very good motto. Typing an angry response is very easy and often tempting, but our actions have consequences. The Internet gives us a big advantage: we can take time to think about the best response.
- Do you get stressed and upset by confrontation in real life? If you do, avoid it online. Online arguments are risky and can leave you feeling extremely distressed, losing sleep and spending hours thinking about how annoyed you are. Walk away before it starts!
- Treasure positive friendships with people who

make you feel good and who you can respond to positively. A few of those are worth far more than 50 contacts you don't really care about.

- Avoid making any public posts when you are feeling emotional, because you won't be thinking clearly. Wait till you're calmer and in control. If you need to talk now, do so privately, with someone you really trust.

- Don't forget that anything you put online will stick around for ever, even if you delete it, so make sure you won't regret that embarrassing photo, status or message in a few years' time!

- Lots of people aren't good at expressing themselves in writing or noticing the tone of their messages. They might sound abrupt or sarcastic without meaning to. Misunderstandings can easily arise like that. If you're not sure what someone meant, check. Don't assume.

- Remember that everyone likes and dislikes different people. If you think someone doesn't like you, stay away from them, offline and online. You'll make your life a lot easier.

SECTION TWO

Making and Managing Friendships

How and why does friendship happen? I don't know, to be honest! I have talked about "chemistry", meaning that something happens at a level beyond our control, making us naturally drawn to some people and not others. Many friendships start and grow really quickly, and both people will say they knew straightaway they would be friends. Other friendships take longer to get going.

Although it usually looks as though you didn't do anything to make a friendship happen, in fact you probably did: by smiling at the right time, saying the "right thing", behaving in a way that the other person liked. Of course, you don't know in advance what the "right thing" is and it's better not to try too hard, because if you do you're not really being yourself. It will be hard to keep trying so hard for long. Better just to be natural and wait to meet people who like the natural you.

As I said in Section One, people tend to become

friends with people who share their values and likes, and who have similar behaviours and emotional reactions. We usually feel comfortable with people who behave similarly to ourselves because it's easier to understand them.

That doesn't mean we can only have friends who are just like us. It's quite possible to be good friends with someone who is different in lots of ways, but even if that happens, you will usually find that there are also many similarities. It would just be too exhausting if you disagreed about everything and that's sometimes why friendships break down.

Lots of friendships start because of a particular shared experience. That's one reason why being the new person at a school can be tough: everyone else has experienced things you weren't part of. But soon you will have had these experiences, whether of annoying teachers, team successes, after-school clubs, school plays or books you read in the reading group. All these things build bonds for you.

"Chemistry" is a good enough way to explain those first moments when you have just met someone and you think, *I like how this person seems – I think we could be friends.* And you fall into conversation easily. But after that, becoming a proper friend requires lots of conversations and interactions, and either the friendship grows because you make each other feel good and secure, or it doesn't. And that's not so much chemistry as finding that you share interests, hobbies, a sense of humour, personality, strengths, values, or any of the things that go to make us each individuals. The more of those things you share, the easier it is to grow that friendship.

How to make good friends

The way we behave affects how others behave towards us. I'm not suggesting it's your fault if someone is mean to you – it's not! But there are things you can do to make it easier to grow good friendships.

First, I'll look at that stage when you don't know the other person (or group) at all and you haven't built any bonds yet, but you think you'd like to. The early stages of a friendship can be daunting, because you aren't sure of the other person and it's so easy to let shyness and self-consciousness get in the way. You might doubt whether they really like you, or you might wish you'd said something different. Relax! It can take time and there's no point in rushing it. Whether friendships grow quickly or take longer doesn't matter in the end.

Then I'll look at how to "manage" those friendships as they grow. And all this without changing any of the wonderful things that make you you!

BE FRIENDLY

I've said that how people behave towards you is not your "fault". But actually, sometimes and in some ways, it can be affected by how you behave. When people treat you badly, it's their fault, not yours, but it's still worth noticing how your behaviour affects others. Understanding this will give you better control over your life and relationships.

It doesn't mean you have to be a different person but if you are aware of how you appear to others and how they react, you can choose what to do. You can stay the same, you can change bits of your behaviour *if you want.*

Let me give you an example. I am easily irritated, but I can also be friendly and warm. How I react to a stranger when I meet them can range from prickly and hostile to warm and welcoming, and the difference is at least partly to do with how they behave. If someone is hostile to me, I will be hostile back – not on purpose, just naturally. If someone crowds my space or interrupts me, they won't get a good reaction. But if someone is friendly to me, I'm likely to be open and smile back.

My point is that people can make me behave in a certain way by behaving in a certain way themselves. I'm not *blaming* them, because I'm the one doing the reacting, and if they don't know me, they can't be expected to know how I'll react. But their behaviour and my reaction are linked.

If you want to make new friends more easily, especially in a situation where you are new, it is a good idea to try to look and sound friendly and warm. You won't very easily make friends if you're looking grumpy, cold and hostile. Sometimes shyness or nervousness can look like hostility so it's worth being aware of your expression.

WHAT IF SMILING IS HARD?

There's something I noticed when I had children of my own and I met lots of small children. Some of them had what I called "open" faces and others had "closed" faces. Some children would make direct eye contact and smile easily; they would respond eagerly to questions from annoying adults; their emotions were clear on their faces. I described them as having "open expressions". Other children tended not to look directly at the eyes of other people, especially adults; they didn't grin or show excitement easily, especially if they knew people were looking; and you couldn't easily tell what they were thinking. They were more reserved. I described their expressions as being more "closed".

If you have a closed expression, people will often tell you to "cheer up". That is so annoying! People used to do that to me and it drove me nuts.

Like other people who've had that experience, I've had to learn to force more expression on to my face. Why should I have to do that, you might ask? Well, one reason is that it creates a warmer atmosphere and helps other people open up. Another reason is that it helps build friendship bonds. If a friend has had good news, it's important to be able to show excitement and pleasure.

So, I think it's a sensible strategy: think about what your face is showing and make sure it's showing what you want it to show.

BE GENEROUS

I don't mean give people presents! I mean be generous with your time, your smiles, kindness and support. I am not suggesting you suck up to people or try to buy their friendship or do anything that feels unnatural. What I'm suggesting is: consider what makes you happy when someone does it for you and think about how you could do the same.

Small acts of kindness have two effects: they benefit the person receiving the kindness but they also have a positive effect on the giver. There's a phrase, "To give is to receive," meaning that when you do something for someone else, you will also get something out of it. There's been lots of research showing that gifts benefit the giver and there are websites dedicated to suggestions of these small acts of kindness. (See Resources.)

PAY ATTENTION TO OTHERS

One very important way of being generous is to pay attention to other people. If you only talk about yourself, it's not likely to make you friends. So, when you're with other people, ask them about themselves. If they say something bad has just happened, don't say, "Oh yes, that happened to me" and then go off into your own story. Make sure you keep listening, because this is their story. If you ask someone a question or for their opinion, listen to their answer.

What if you're not really interested in other people? Well, frankly, you may need to pretend. Because if you're not interested in them, why should they be interested in you?

I'll talk about being a good listener when I talk about how to manage your friendships, but I want to mention it here, too, because it's very important at the stage of making new friends. Having a conversation is a two-way thing: listening and talking. The irony is that people who find talking difficult often get so stressed about it that they end up talking too much and forgetting to listen and ask others about themselves.

BE POSITIVE

Of course, you don't always feel positive. After all, if you're upset or stressed about your friendship situations, that will be making you feel negative, perhaps overwhelmingly so. But if you can possibly put on a more positive face with people you're trying to get to know, you may find it helps in many ways. For a start, the act of smiling and trying to look positive can actually have the effect of improving how you feel. Using your smiling muscles releases endorphins (often called "happy chemicals") in your brain, boosting your mood. Watching a funny video will have the same effect.

The other big effect of keeping a positive face in front of other people is that they are more likely to be drawn to you. Now, a major word of caution: I am not suggesting you make a habit of hiding your sadness or worries. Bottling them up for too long is not a healthy way to deal with bad feelings; telling them to friends is a good idea and is a proper part of friendship. What I am saying is that when you're first getting to know someone – building those bonds – then you will find it easier if you can at least sometimes show your positive side.

You might find it helpful to talk about your worries and sadness with an adult or someone else you know, instead of when you're trying to build a brand-new friendship. Then, once you've developed the friendship, you'll be able to share more with your friend or friends, because you'll know that you want to support each other.

TAKE PART IN AN ACTIVITY IN SCHOOL

This isn't about how you behave and appear but some practical things you can *do*. In your classroom, you are thrown together with a load of people you haven't chosen. What if you could narrow that down a bit to people who have a shared interest? Is there a club for singing, yoga, reading, dance, sport, art, pottery, anything you fancy? It can be scary joining something but it really is a great way to make friends easily, because you don't have to make conversation: you're all there to do whatever activity it is, and conversation is secondary.

When you first join the activity, just introduce yourself

to someone by saying what your name is and asking them theirs. Don't be upset if they don't respond well straightaway: they may be shy or you might just have picked the wrong person! Try again with someone else. Start with really basic questions, such as asking them how long they've been doing this activity, what the teacher is like, whether it's easy. Or admire something they've done.

START A HOBBY OUTSIDE SCHOOL

A hobby is good for your mental health, wellbeing and mood; it helps make you into a rounded, more interesting person; it's a valuable stress relief, taking you away from your daily worries or schoolwork; and it can bring opportunities to make friends with the same interests. There are countless hobbies to choose from. It could be collecting things; or something creative, such as making music, art or writing; or talking about things, such as books, films or video games; or active, like sailing, climbing or dancing.

There's bound to be something happening in your area. Or, if there isn't anything that interests you, try online. (Make sure your group includes people of your own age and remember all the safety checks about communicating online.)

Some hobbies might seem "solitary" – creative writing, for example – but you can still meet other people with the same interest and chat about your hobby.

START SOMETHING!

If there isn't an activity already set up that suits you, why not start your own group? You could put a notice up in school to see if anyone would be interested – or maybe get one person interested first and then put the notice up together. Here are some ideas:

- Do you sing or play an instrument? See if anyone wants to start a group or band.
- Do you write poetry or stories? How about starting a writing group, a magazine or a blog? You might get a teacher or librarian to help.
- Enjoy acting or singing? See if you can get people together and perform a play, musical or concert. It doesn't have to be to do with school: you could perform for an old people's home, a playgroup or a children's hospital.
- Start a "Small acts of kindness" club or a Happiness club.
- Is there a problem in your community that you'd like to deal with? Bullying? Vandalism? A park that needs attention or a clean-up? Get some people together to deal with it.

How to keep your friendships strong

Once you've made friendships, how do you keep them strong? All the things I mentioned previously will be relevant: listening, being positive, etc. But there are other things to think about, too.

A really strong friendship can survive for a long time without much attention. Adults often comment that they have a small number of friends who they can go without contacting for years, but then when they meet "it's as though we were never apart". But most friendships are not like that. If you don't do things to build and strengthen the bonds, the bonds will usually fade. That's why it's hard to manage a lot of friendships: there just aren't enough hours in the day.

So, even if you're a reserved person and find active socialising tiring, make sure you keep some contact going, whether it's via text or social media or in person. Of course, if you're particularly busy or something's going on in your life, you can tell a friend that you're not able to do stuff together for a while.

Social media is fine, but face-to-face is really good at strengthening friendships, as I described in Section One. Suggest a cinema trip, café meeting, chilling at your house. But if you and your friend prefer just the occasional contact, that's no problem: as long as you're both getting what you want from the friendship.

BE A GOOD LISTENER

A good listener is a valuable friend. Good listening means putting your own feelings aside as you give proper attention to the other person. It means not judging but accepting that the person's feelings are valid. So, if they say they are sad or scared or angry about something, you don't say, "It's silly to feel like that." If your friend is going through something you've never experienced, you don't say, "I know how you feel" – because, actually, you don't. You say something like, "That sounds so difficult – I guess you must be feeling XXX." And then you can show sympathy by saying, "I'm really sorry you're going through this", or whatever is appropriate to the situation.

Even professional counselling is mostly about good listening. The "core conditions" are understanding, acceptance and genuineness. A counsellor has to understand how their client is feeling, accept it and genuinely want to help them. You can do that as a friend.

What if you don't know what to say when someone tells you something? Don't worry! You don't have to have a clever or deep answer. You might say something like, "I'm so sorry. I wish I could make you feel better" or "That must be awful – I'm really sorry" or even "I don't know what to say – is there anything I can do to help?" All those things show the person that you listened, that you care, that you didn't judge, that you didn't dismiss their emotions as being ridiculous.

SHOULD YOU EVER LIE TO A FRIEND?

Maybe. We usually praise honesty as a virtue, but honesty can be hurtful or pointless or both. When honesty is either of those things, I believe it's wrong.

If you're at the stage of making new friends, you shouldn't feel you have to risk that by telling someone you don't like their hair/outfit/shoes/new phone, even if they ask. OK, so I don't think you have to say you love something when you don't, but you can usually find a way to say nothing. Or reply in a way that doesn't reveal much. Why risk hurting someone or making them angry when there's nothing to be gained for either of you?

It's harder with close friends, when one of them asks you directly for your opinion. Then I think you have to work out whether they really want your opinion, to help them make a choice, for instance. Or whether they just want validation. If they really want your opinion, you can say, "Well, OK, this is just my opinion, but I think X would look better – but why don't we ask someone else because I could be wrong?"

Being tactful is part of building friendships. I have lots of friends who are writers. If I don't like their book, I don't tell them. If I can think of something positive and truthful to say, I will. But I won't say I didn't like it. Why spoil a friendship and my friend's self-esteem just for the sake of being honest? It's not kind and it's not helpful. After all, it's usually just personal opinion, not fact.

Teachers, coaches, doctors and others are paid to be honest. It's their job. It's only a friend's job to be honest when it's necessary, helpful and kind.

I think the best thing is to ask yourself: if this were the other way round, what would I want from my friend? How much honesty? How much sensitivity?

SAYING SORRY

Everyone makes mistakes. Sometimes we say the wrong thing. We can accidentally hurt our friends. Or we might even hurt them on purpose, if we are angry with them. (I'm not saying that's right but you know it can happen.) Saying sorry – and meaning it – almost always solves the problem completely or at least makes it much better.

You do have to mean it and look as though you mean it, though. Do you remember being forced to apologize for something when you were a child? Maybe you'd hit another child or you'd grabbed their toy and made them cry? And an adult told you to say sorry. You didn't want to, perhaps because you were angry with the other child because they'd started it, or maybe because you were embarrassed. Eventually, you were forced to say sorry. And you didn't feel any better, because you didn't mean it. The other child might have realized you didn't mean it, so they didn't feel better either.

That is not a useful apology. A proper apology, where you really regret what you did – even if you couldn't help

65

it and it was a genuine mistake – and where it's really obvious to the other person that you regret it, is entirely different. It's one of the most important moments in a friendship; the moment that can often heal and strengthen the bonds.

It can be difficult to pluck up the courage to say sorry but it's worth doing. I've seen adults suggest to each other that apologizing is a sign of weakness. I completely disagree with this! Apologizing when you've done anything you wish you hadn't, whether genuinely by mistake or just at a time of anger, is strong, practical, effective and powerful.

If, however, your friend doesn't accept the apology, your friendship will have a problem. You might try again later, when the other person has calmed down, but if they won't accept the apology I am not sure there's much more you can or should do. Maybe this is a friendship that wasn't meant to last.

Very often when arguments happen and friendships are in danger, no one says sorry. Then, people either carry on with life pretending it never happened – but one person is left feeling resentful – or the friendship ends up being properly damaged.

GIVING PEOPLE SPACE

Most people need time alone sometimes. If your friend is more introverted than you, they will need more space than you. (I'll be talking a lot more about introversion in Section Four.) By "space", I mean the possibility of being on your own for a while. Don't take this as a rejection: it's not about you but about their legitimate needs. If you're not sure what your friend feels about this, you can ask! Ask if they like spending time alone sometimes; or if you're suggesting doing something together at the weekend, be sensitive to whether perhaps they are wanting to say, "No, I really want to do some stuff on my own" but are maybe too embarrassed to say so.

DEALING WITH JEALOUSY

Lots of friendships and relationships are spoiled by one person being too jealous. Jealousy is perfectly natural – especially if someone feels insecure in themselves – but it's very destructive. And there are so many opportunities in school situations for jealousy amongst friends: when you see your friend having fun with someone else, sharing a secret, or making an arrangement to meet up and not asking you, for example.

We all need to realize that we cannot be the only person in someone's life. Do you only want one friend or do you want several? Do you find that you need different people for different reasons – one for having a laugh with, another for having a moan with, others because they know what's going on in your family? Well, that's how it is for most people: we need a range of friends at different times. Try not to expect to be The One.

If you do find that you're having major feelings of jealousy about one or more friends, that your stomach clenches when you see a friend laughing and chatting with someone else, you need to think carefully: is this because you have problems of insecurity or is your friend really starting another friendship that means your existing friendship will suffer?

If it's the first, I recommend you talk to an adult about your lack of self-esteem.

But if it's the second, I suggest you step back, give it time, and see how things seem in a few weeks. Meanwhile, spend time with someone else – not to try to upset your friend but to remind yourself that you don't only have one friend. You might well be overreacting, though, as emotions often cloud judgement. If you're not sure, you could ask another friend, but do this carefully: make certain it's someone you can really trust, or else ask in such a way that they won't know who you are talking about. The last thing you want is to make things worse. If you can't do this, I recommend you just wait and see how the situation changes. You'll soon work out how correct you were. And if it turns out that your friend is really moving away from you, then you'll need either to find a way to talk to them about it or just let this friendship go. You don't have to hang around feeling excluded.

THAT TWO-WAY FRIENDSHIP THING

I talked about this in Section One but it's worth saying again: friendship shouldn't be one-sided. If one person is doing all the giving and the other all the taking, that's not a recipe for a strong friendship.

If you're doing all the taking, think about whether this is temporary (perhaps because you have something going on that needs extra help from friends) or longer term. If it's temporary, let your friend know that you realize you're taking a lot of their time right now and that you really appreciate it. Tell them you're very sorry if it seems to be making you selfish, but as soon as you're through it, you will be there for them, too.

If my question has made you look at yourself and realize, *Wow – actually I do seem to demand a lot from my friends and I don't give much back*, then what can you do about it? A lot! And if you do, your friendship bonds will be stronger and you will have helped both yourself and your friends. So, take steps now to show that you care.

What if you feel you're doing all the giving? Again, think about whether this is temporary, because your friend is going through a rough patch. If it is, this is part of friendship. If your friend has a mental health problem, you may be frustrated that you keep giving the same advice and it doesn't seem to help: this is a common aspect of illnesses such as depression. It can be frustrating, of course, but if you are a good friend, you will probably continue to want to help, even though it's hard.

Sometimes you might feel that you can't go on being the giver all the time. You have your own needs. My advice here is to value other friendships. This doesn't mean you have to desert your friend in need, just that you can enjoy benefits of different friendships as well. If the friend who is suffering makes it difficult for you to have other friends, you need to find a good time to talk to them and say something along the lines of, "I am your friend and I care about you, but it's also really normal that I have other friends and sometimes I need to be with them. But that doesn't mean I don't care about you. I can help you better if I can also look after myself."

There's a saying that you can't help other people if you don't care for yourself. Being a good friend does not mean neglecting your own needs. If you do too much for other people and don't balance this with doing things for yourself, you may end up feeling bitter. If you need time to do something on your own, or your friend hasn't noticed that you're upset or stressed, say so. Pick your moment and do it as sensitively as you can.

HELPING WITH PROBLEMS

Following on from the previous point, what if your friend needs help that you can't provide? There are lots of ways this can happen but I think they divide into two types of problem: (1) When you've already done all you can but your friend doesn't accept the help or follow the advice. (2) When the problem feels too big, too difficult and too serious, or you don't have all the information you need to be able to help.

With the first type: you tried. You did your best and it's not your fault if your friend doesn't or can't accept your advice. Obviously, you might keep trying but you can't do that for ever. At some point, you may just have to say (either to yourself or to your friend) that you've done all you can but that you'll still always be there for them. Sometimes that's the best thing anyway, just being there for them to turn to.

With the second type: recognize that some things are too big for you to deal with. Most adults would find them difficult, too. Some adults spend years training as counsellors to help people with deep or difficult problems, whether emotional, psychological, physical or practical. So, you shouldn't feel bad if you don't know how to help.

If you have a friend going through really difficult times, you need to do two things. First, strongly encourage them to talk to an adult. Reassure them that there will be strategies to help. Remind them that they can go to a GP and talk in complete confidence about any medical or psychological issue, and the GP won't tell parents without agreement. Also remind them that Childline (see Resources) offers 100% confidentiality.

Second, let them know that, even though you

personally don't know what to do to make the problem better, you are there for them and are their friend.

BEING LOYAL

Good friends don't go round bad-mouthing each other behind their backs. Good friends don't scheme against each other. On the other hand, everyone makes mistakes and people in groups sometimes behave in a way they wouldn't on their own. So, for example, if you're in a group of people and someone says something mean about another friend who happens not to be there, you might find yourself going along with the crowd and not sticking up for them. That's not great and next time you see your friend, you will probably feel bad. But it's not the end of the world! You made a mistake and, if you recognize that, you will try not to do it again. If you can let your friend know that you feel bad and wish you'd acted differently, that will help.

As with so many things, it's a matter of thinking what you'd want to happen if people were talking about you: you'd want your friend to stick up for you. So, that's how you should ideally behave if you have the opportunity. It's not always easy, though, and you do need to consider your own safety.

If you discover that a friend of yours has bad-mouthed you or not stuck up for you, you have a right to challenge them. But understand that they will probably react negatively because no one likes being caught out. You might prefer to leave it, if you can move on and forget about it. Or you might be able to let your friend know that you know, but without making it a big deal. After all, they might be feeling bad and welcome the chance to explain. It's very hard to advise without knowing the circumstances, but there's one thing I can be fairly certain about: even if it seems very intense just now, that feeling will fade.

KEEPING SECRETS

Secrets are dangerous things! Problems and huge arguments can happen when someone doesn't keep a secret – and often it needs real willpower not to. It can be so tempting. Sometimes it can be hard to avoid when you're asked about it directly and you either have to tell a lie – which involves extreme powers of acting – or give away the secret or refuse to give it up. If you give away a friend's secret that's not only disloyal but risky, because if they find out, they're going to be furious. But refusing when someone is asking is difficult. If possible, stand firm, perhaps explaining that you've been sworn to secrecy and you just can't give away someone else's secret. But there's no doubt that these situations are very tricky. If you've already made a mistake like that, don't beat yourself up about it. One day it will be forgotten.

What if the secret is one you really feel you ought to tell for the sake of someone's safety and wellbeing? Let's look at some real-life possibilities:

- You have discovered a friend self-harming; the friend swears you to secrecy. I think: Your friend needs help. But you need to make him realize this, so that he gives you permission to tell someone, or, even better, agrees to tell someone himself. Explain that you care and are really worried but that it's too big a thing for you to help with.

- You discover that a friend of yours is two-timing her boyfriend. (Obviously, the same applies to any gender.) She swears you to secrecy. I think: This should not be your problem. It is not your job to tell the boyfriend. But it might be your job to show your friend that you don't think it's right and that you don't want to know any more about it; also that she should make up her mind between the two. But what if the boyfriend is a good friend of yours? This is trickier but I still think it's not your business, or at least not at first. If your friend doesn't stop pretty quickly, you're going to have to choose between your friend and the other friend she's cheating on. Although it's not your fault, it has become your problem. You might want to ask someone else for advice, without naming names.

- You discover that a friend of yours is involved in something bad – maybe criminal, such as shoplifting. This is *very* tricky! Legally, if you know a crime has been committed, you have to tell someone, but that's much easier said than done. It's beyond difficult to do that when it's a friend involved. I think: In this situation you could find a way to ask an adult what you should do, but not being specific or giving names, just saying, "Supposing someone had done this and I knew about it...?" A word of caution: if you "disclose" a crime or potential crime to a responsible adult, they can't ignore it; they have to take it seriously and that may mean reporting it to the authorities. So be very careful what you disclose. On the other hand, sharing the problem with an adult is most often the best thing to do. Again, it's very hard to advise without knowing the circumstances. If you have no one to pass the responsibility on to, an organisation like Childline (see Resources) would give good advice.

Unfortunately, as I say, secrets can be difficult and may sometimes damage friendships. But it's important to remember that everyone has secrets and they are harmless in themselves. They only become a problem when the wrong people find out about them.

You're bound to make mistakes with this at some point, but my main advice is that when you've promised to keep something secret, do it, as long as what you're keeping secret is not illegal or harmful to anyone. Don't be tempted to pass it to someone else, saying, "Promise you won't tell?" Because why wouldn't they? After all, you did...

Staying friends

A friendship is like a plant: you have to nurture it. You can't just watch it or forget about it. Other animals do things to nurture their friendships, too. Apes groom each other by picking fleas out of their fur. Dogs and cats lick each other. I'm not suggesting you do these things to your friends – you'd be breaking some human social rules if you did! What humans do instead is talk; hang out with each other; give each other time and attention.

Every time you give your friends even a few seconds of your attention, you build bonds. If you don't, the bonds weaken. As I said earlier, once you have a very strong friendship, it is possible to go for ages without contact, and when you meet the person again the friendship picks up where it left off. But that usually only works for a really strong bond. More often, "losing touch" means weakening the friendship and sometimes losing it.

The fact that friendship needs effort, nurturing and some form of contact becomes interesting when you remember what I said about the number of "friends" you might have on social media: hundreds. And how you can't give attention to that many people. Social media companies have come up with instant ways of making that contact – for example, by clicking "like" on someone's photo – but it's still hard to grow real friendships simply by doing things like this.

There are really no shortcuts to nurturing and keeping friends: we have to spend actual time and effort. We have to let our friends know we're there, that we're still their friend, that we like spending time with them. We don't have to do it all the time, or every day, but we have to do it enough. We can do it in small ways, often, or in bigger ways less often. For example, we can send a few short messages quite frequently, or we can occasionally do something "bigger", like meeting for coffee, going to the cinema, shopping, watching a match together.

Good friends can fall out sometimes, but it doesn't mean the friendship is weak or will break. Sometimes a falling-out does become permanent, of course, depending on all sorts of different reasons. But in a strong friendship you can make mistakes and say sorry. As long as the apology is genuine and the other person accepts it, the friendship can get back on track. But if not, remember: not all friendships are meant to last and you will often need to move on and make new ones.

WILL WE BE FRIENDS FOR EVER?

It's impossible to know whether you and any of your friends will be friends permanently. One of the best feelings is when a friendship feels so strong that it must last for ever. But things change in ways you can't predict. You and your friends will change. That might not matter and perhaps you will still remain friends, but many factors can stop that happening. My advice is don't overthink it. Don't try to predict. Enjoy the friendships you have. Value what they give you in terms of pleasure and trust and fun and happiness, and just don't think about the future.

Many adults say that their current friends are not the ones they had at school, even though at the time they couldn't imagine losing touch with them. The friendships we all need are ones we have now, the people we can call on now, whose lives are entwined with our lives now. At each stage we can make new friends; we can keep our old ones, too, but if some or all of those older friendships fade and stop being part of our daily lives, that's entirely normal.

One of the many great things about the Internet and social media is that we can always reconnect with old friends if we want to. Those options are there: we do not have to lose touch. But we often do and it's not something to be sad about. It's partly, as I say, because we all change and partly because we simply can't manage more friend-ships than we have time and energy for.

QUIZ

Are you a good friend?

Friendship thrives on both sides treating each other well. If you really like your friend, you'll probably want to do things for them, but it can sometimes be hard because you have your own life to lead and your own problems to deal with. Friendship does involve generosity and I think it's important to get a good balance of being generous to your friends and yet still caring for yourself.

Give yourself a score of 0, 1, 2, 3 or 4, depending on how strongly you agree with the following statements: 0 for "not at all", 4 for "extremely".

1. I think I'm a good listener and I am patient when friends are telling me their problems.
2. If I realize I've not treated a friend well, I take steps to put it right and I'd be anxious if I didn't.
3. I try hard to compliment my friends because it makes them feel good.
4. If my friend wins a prize or is selected for something instead of me, I'm very pleased for them. OK, I might wish it was me, just for a moment, but then I'm happy for them.
5. If one of my friends is being teased or victimised, I will do

my best to stand up for them and help them.

6. People often come to me with problems because they know they can trust me and that I'll do my best to help them.

7. I feel that I'm a supportive friend and this is really important to me.

8. I often do things for my friends without them asking me to.

9. I love helping my friends.

10. I often stop myself from telling a friend about something good that's happened to me because I know they're going through a bad patch.

11. If a friend has just had a break-up and is really upset, I'll spend as much time as necessary listening and helping, even if I have problems of my own.

12. If my friend accidentally says something hurtful to me, I put up with it because I don't want to spoil our friendship.

13. If my friend really wanted to do something and I didn't, I'd do what they wanted rather than what I wanted.

14. I have a friend who makes it difficult or impossible for me to have other friends, but that's OK because I know this friend needs me.

15. Sometimes I feel really dragged down by trying to help my friends, but I think it's important to carry on because that's what friends are for.

This set of questions has a trick behind it: if you have

scored very highly – say, above 40 out of 60 – I would ask you to take a closer look at which questions you picked up most points on. If you scored highly on questions 10 and 11, that's OK as long as you don't do this too much and ignore your own needs. If you scored lots of points on question 12 onwards, you may be doing too much for others and not looking after yourself. Remember what I said about two-way friendships and how friendships need to work for everyone concerned?

Take a look at the questions you scored 4 on and ask yourself whether you might sometimes be sacrificing yourself too much. Doing things for friends and going the extra mile are important and positive things, but not if that goes too far. If a friend is taking a great deal of your emotional energy, think about whether you can share this role with someone else.

Never forget to be generous to yourself, too.

When friendships go wrong

They often do and it's always hard at the time. Depending on what happened, it can really affect your self-esteem, at least at first. At school, people will take sides, talking about whose "fault" it is and sticking up for one side or the other, often without knowing all the facts.

Obviously, every friendship and every break-up is different and I wouldn't be able to explain them all in this book. The next section will suggest lots of fascinating things that can influence friendships and behaviour. But very often, you won't know what the cause was.

You might spend a lot of time wondering why it went wrong or whose fault it was. You might spend a lot of time being angry or sad. Maybe you feel angry if your ex-friend behaved badly, or ashamed if you did. Or you could be embarrassed if it was all very public. You might feel humiliated if you feel people are looking at you and sneering, or deliberately ignoring you.

Whoever's fault it was, or even if it was no one's fault, it's not pleasant. But that feeling won't last for long. You might find it awkward being in the same room as the other person, but at some point you'll both get sick of being hostile and the awkwardness or anger will fade. Especially if you carry on behaving like a decent person.

Think of the phrase "the moral high ground". It means being in a position where you know you're behaving well, even if someone else isn't. It's much more comfortable than knowing that you're behaving badly, I promise! Knowing you've done something wrong or that you're being spiteful is not good for the soul. If someone else is doing that, more fool them, but don't let it happen to you.

Rise above it and stay strong. You might feel you can't face going into school but it's really important to go in – and the sooner the better. It's like falling off a horse: you have to get back on straight away, otherwise it gets harder and harder. If you handle it right, every day it will get a little easier. Nothing will be as bad as the first day.

Try to avoid saying spiteful things just to score points. You could make it even worse or take longer to get through it. Just hold your breath, keep your mouth firmly closed and walk past in a dignified way. You may not think you're winning but you are, because most people realize that staying silent is the harder, tougher, braver thing to do.

I'm not saying you have to put up with bad treatment or unfair behaviour, of course. If you want to, you can report it, but if the circumstances allow you to keep that moral high ground, it will usually be the best way in the end.

KNOW WHAT'S RIGHT FOR YOU

When we get tangled up in emotions, we can end up doing things which, if we planned them in advance, we wouldn't do. Humans are impulsive and we are ruled by our emotions so much of the time. But try to take a moment to pause and think, *How does this feel to me?* If you're going through a difficult period with friends and peers, it's easy to feel you have to do certain things to keep them on your side. But does it feel right if that means joining a group who treat others badly, or who make you be something you're not? Be confident in your own morals and that little voice of conscience which tells you, if you listen, that doing the wrong things to get friends won't help in the end.

WHAT IF YOUR FRIENDSHIP HASN'T ENDED YET BUT YOU'RE WORRIED IT'S GOING TO?

You've been friends with this person for years and you thought your relationship was going to last for ever, but it feels like it's fading. What can you do?

I don't think you should do anything very much – unless, of course, you think *you've* been doing something wrong. Maybe you've been going through a really bad experience and you haven't had the headspace to spend time with your friend. Well, you can put that right if you want to.

Ask yourself why you think this friendship is fading. Do you feel bad vibes from your friend suddenly or think that they are spending more time with someone else? Because each situation is different, I can't really advise you on a particular friendship but what I will say is this: don't be too quick to judge. You might be right but it might just be a phase.

If these bad vibes have started quite recently, perhaps you've done something and you didn't realize? Could you ask? You never know: it could be something simple. Or it could be a complete misunderstanding. Or nothing at all. If your friend says it's nothing, leave it: you can't keep asking what's wrong, or it will become annoying and probably not improve the friendship.

If you really feel that you and your friend have been growing apart over a period of time, I don't think you should or can really do anything about it. You'd have to both want to. I think it's best to let it drift and go your own ways, ideally without a big falling-out. You might make contact years later and your friendship might pick up again. Friendships do change, fade and disappear.

Move on. There's a huge wide world out there, with billions of people in it. And some of them will be good friends to you.

* * *

Not fitting in – being "different"

This is an incredibly big thing for many young people and might be the main reason you've chosen to read the book. Not fitting in can feel horrible. Now you know why belonging to a group is important to humans. On the other hand, some people thrive on being different and choose to dress or act without taking any notice of what other people think. Good for them! But probably it's fair to say that most people find it difficult, at least in some ways and some of the time. So, if you're struggling with not fitting in, you are not alone. (Remember that actually everyone is different!)

At the beginning of the book, I mentioned my own experience of not fitting in. So I do understand what it can be like, though everyone's experiences will vary. It can lead to teasing, excluding and bullying. A very common and deeply unpleasant example happens when people make you feel you can't sit with them at lunch. (This is so important that I've added some information in Resources.) Being on the receiving end of such behaviour is horrible. No one likes it. But the main thing to remember is that it's not your fault. It's the fault of the people behaving meanly, cruelly or thoughtlessly.

Very often they just aren't thinking. Perhaps they haven't even tried to see how you might be feeling. They might be doing it to go along with the group – and I'll talk more about group behaviour later. It can also be to make themselves feel stronger, bigger, and to strengthen their position within the group. Or they could be reflecting prejudices they've learnt at home or elsewhere. So, lots of different reasons might be behind their behaviour.

It's also possible that they see you as a threat. You might find it hard to believe that you could be a threat to a group of apparently confident people. But supposing there's something about you that they feel threatened by: you're clever; you seem strong on the outside (even if inside you're shaking); you're not a conformist (someone who follows the crowd and always tries to fit in); you've got some kind of special skill – in music or academic work. Any of these things can challenge their need to be "top dog".

People react to all kinds of difference. It could be a disability; something particular about your voice/height/size; your ethnic origin, skin colour or religion. If you are questioning your gender identity or sexuality, or if you dress or act differently from how people expect you to dress or act, that, too, can be something that they may pick on you for – at least until they understand. One set of individuals who often have difficulty fitting in are people with Asperger syndrome. Asperger's is not an illness but it consists of a different way of seeing the world and difficulty in working out social behaviours and following the "rules" of interacting with others. Obviously, no one should be judgemental about any of the natural differences between humans, but it's an unfortunate fact that some people do react in an unfriendly way when they meet someone different from them. (I have included a few things that might help you in Resources.)

Remember this important fact, though: many people are not judgemental, but warm and positive. In this book I've tended to highlight negative behaviour, because it's partly a book about solving problems. But most people are good at heart. Most people don't actively want to hurt you, though it's completely understandable if the ones you notice most are the ones who are making your life difficult. Some of those people aren't mean underneath: they've done or said things they shouldn't have through thoughtlessness, ignorance, or whatever. Many will learn to be better, with education and time to grow up.

Teasing, harassment or bullying for any reason are obviously wrong. So, what can you do about it if it's happening to you?

Let me say first that you don't have to do anything if you don't want to. The people inflicting this behaviour on you are the ones who should change, not you. You aren't doing anything wrong, so you don't have to change your behaviour in any way. But what if you want to? I think it's important to feel you don't have to act on your own: you can ask for help and support from the many good adults and young people who will be on your side.

If the behaviour is happening in school, that is the best place to start looking for support. Some schools are much better than others at dealing with all forms of bullying and harassment, but they should have a written policy that gives you ways to get help and support.

If the behaviour is not happening in school (and even if it is), you can choose from various people to talk to: a friend; a parent or other relative; a teacher (even if it's not happening in school, a teacher may be able to advise); or the experts in one of the online organisations, such as Childline, YoungMinds and Bullying UK, that help people who are being bullied, harassed or victimised (see Resources).

If you belong to a particular group of people – for example, if you have a specific disability or illness, if you are in the Lesbian, Gay, Bisexual, Trans and Queer (LGBTQ) community or have been a victim of racism – you will find advice on the websites that serve that particular group. If you don't yet know of such groups, ask at your library or do an online search. It would also be great if you could find a local group of young people in the same sort of situation or with the same concerns and issues as you.

The support is out there and there are many sympathetic people of all ages who will want to help and to stop the negative behaviour of others.

"Difference" makes many people uncomfortable. Well,

they need to think about it and then get over it. Don't feel you need to hide your difference, even if you could. Yes, it will present you with challenges, but one day I hope you'll look back with pride and realize that they made you a stronger person. One day, you'll find a group of people who value you for who you are. People of all ages can be hostile, judgemental and ignorant, but you'll also find more people who are welcoming, positive, sensible and decent human beings.

BEING THE NEWBIE

It can be really difficult if you arrive at a school when everyone else has already made their friendship groups. You might feel like an outsider for quite a long time, and people sometimes don't realize how you feel and might not help you integrate. Something as apparently simple as finding a person to sit with at lunch is very important to how comfortable and welcomed you feel, and people often don't make that easy at all, whether through thoughtlessness or meanness.

The main thing to remember is that this is a *very* common experience. Loads of people have to change schools at various times and for various reasons. And it's always nerve-wracking, even for the most confident person who finds it easy to make new friendship groups.

Although being the newbie is hard, it's also something that can have a really positive effect on the person you become, because it can give you extra empathy – which will help you make friends and be a well-liked person later.

But, at the time, when you're trying to find a way into teenage groups, it's tough.

If you possibly can, try to rise above any silly behaviour by such people. I don't mean to suggest it's easy or that you're wrong to feel uncomfortable and anxious about it. But if you can be strong for a while, you soon won't be the newbie and people will forget that you were.

See if you can find someone else who seems to be outside things – maybe another new person. Talk to them and you might end up becoming friends with them – you never know.

And persevere. Don't give up too early. Don't think, *I'll never settle in.* Most of all, don't try to run away or skip school to avoid the horrible feeling of being the outsider. It will get better, I promise. I can't promise how quickly, but in the meantime try some of the advice in the chapter on "How to make Good Friends".

THINGS TO THINK ABOUT

- Lots of people identify with the feeling of not fitting in. It's a common experience and there will be people around you who feel they don't fit in, even if you think they do.
- People tend to make their first judgement on physical appearance, so looking different can be

92

a challenge at first. But soon people will see beyond appearance to much more important things.

- Whether you're new to the school or you're finding it hard to fit in for any reason, don't forget my earlier tips about making friends and managing friendships.

- School is not for ever – though it might seem like it right now! – and in the "real world" you'll have much more choice about who you spend time with.

- You are changing all the time: that's such a positive thing to hold on to. You may even find that in a year or two, you have more control over who you are and who you want to be. For now, you are still "becoming" and turning into a new you.

- Celebrate your difference! It shows real strength and bravery.

- Being self-conscious is a big deal for teenagers, as you often think everyone's judging you all the time. Well, yes, some people do spend a lot of time judging, but most of the time they are not thinking about you. They are thinking about themselves.

- Being new never lasts long!

- Don't focus on wanting to be part of a big group.

A small group is often preferable. It's less likely to lead to conflict and bad behaviour. So, if you have one or two friends to hang out with, that's your group. You're in!

- Most of all, remember this: people who are unwelcoming to newcomers are the ones with a problem or a fault, not you. If you show them that you are just a decent human and they still reject you, more fool them. They're not going to feel great about it later.

QUIZ

How self-conscious are you?

It's perfectly normal to feel that everyone's looking at you. Occasionally, of course, they are. If you're doing a talk to the class, for example, they obviously are. But if you make a mistake, they won't spend the rest of the day thinking, *Ha ha, Sophie messed up*. Only you will.

But some people are more affected than others by this feeling of exposure. This is when the perfectly normal self-consciousness can get in the way of your confidence to talk to people and relax with them. It could even be that your sense of "not fitting in" is entirely imagined and caused partly by this self-consciousness.

Self-consciousness and social embarrassment are also a bigger deal for teenagers, on average, than for adults. It's one of your brain differences: the areas that are active when teens are embarrassed are more active (and sometimes in different areas) than in adults when facing the same type of awkward situation. (See Resources for more on this.)

We have to deal with people looking at us. We have to learn to put it in perspective and not let it stop us doing things. Let's see how you do on that.

Give yourself a score of 0, 1, 2, 3 or 4, depending on how strongly you think the following statements apply to you: 0 for "not at all", 4 for "extremely".

1. I spend ages deciding whether to put my hand up in class and I test what I'm about to say inside my head first.
2. When I walk along the corridor at school, I feel everyone looks at me and is judging me.
3. If I make a small but silly mistake – such as saying the wrong word – I feel mortified and I keep thinking about it for the rest of the day.
4. When I talk in front of a group of people, I go red.
5. When I am saying something to a group or in public, I feel so obvious and clumsy.
6. I hate standing up if everyone else is sitting down, so I avoid doing something in front of my class.
7. There's something about my face or body that I hate and I would do anything possible to hide it if I could.
8. If there was some medical treatment to make me less self-conscious, I would definitely try this.
9. If I had a superpower, it would be the ability to become invisible.
10. Before a party I will always check what everyone else is wearing, because the idea of turning up wearing the wrong thing would make me feel *so* embarrassed.
11. I can't bear being laughed at – it's one of the worst things for me.

12. I hate it when it's my turn in a game or activity.
13. When I think people are looking at me, my mouth goes dry and I feel sweaty. I panic and don't say sensible things. Then afterwards I'm furious with myself.
14. I check my face and clothes a lot in case there's something embarrassing.
15. I can think of times when I've said no to something because I couldn't face people looking at me.

If you scored very highly on this quiz – over 45, for example – you might benefit from some help. Being too self-conscious is really a form of anxiety and the same strategies help for both. Counselling is a suggestion, but it can be expensive and there is often a waiting list. If you talk to a sensible adult, they will help you face your fears and manage the anxiety a little at a time. These feelings do fade over time, if we face them and take steps to control our responses. Our body can learn to reduce the unpleasant feelings and we can even start to love the things we used to hate. One thing is for sure: you do not want to spend your life overwhelmed by self-consciousness. Most people don't, and, as I said, it's more common for teenagers so you really might just "grow out of it". But if you need or would like help, ask. Even a doctor can help.

SECTION THREE

Empathy

Empathy is the ability to understand and share what another person is feeling. It is something that humans do far, far better than any other animal, and some people are better at it than others.

Not everyone would agree that other mammals have any empathy at all. Obviously it's hard to know what goes on in the "mind" of another animal, or what they feel, because we don't share language. And it's a mistake to think that just because an animal seems upset when another animal is hurt, for example, it means they have real empathy. It's also a mistake to assume that another animal would feel the same as us when a bad thing happens.

For a start, humans have knowledge that other animals don't, which affects how we feel. For example, writing and technology allow us to know things about the past, about people we've never met, and to have some understanding of what will or might happen in the future – and our feelings are influenced by that information. We have a vast amount of knowledge that has an impact on how scared, happy, sad or angry we feel and gives us a wider range of emotions. So, while animals can presumably experience fear of an immediate danger, it's hard to see how they could be afraid of what might happen tomorrow, or whether that headache is a symptom of meningitis, or how they might feel if they fail at whatever challenge is coming up. They might feel something like "sadness" – perhaps when a group member dies – but they can't feel the range of and reasons for sadness that a human might feel.

Robin Dunbar is one of a number of scientists who has measured something called Theory of Mind (ToM – see Resources). Theory of Mind means understanding that what you think or know may not be the same as what I think or know. There are different levels of Theory of Mind. Humans develop the first level at around age three or four. Scientists can test this using the "Sally–Anne" method. A researcher shows a child two dolls called Sally and Anne, and the researcher uses them to act out a scene: Sally hides an object behind a chair. Anne leaves the room. Sally moves the object while Anne is out of the room. Anne comes back. The researcher then asks the child, "Where does Anne think the doll is?" A child who has developed the first level of ToM will know that *Anne still thinks the doll is where it was first put.* A child who hasn't developed this will believe that Anne realizes that the doll is *where the child knows it is*. That child hasn't learnt that different minds know and believe different things.

Researchers have devised tests to see whether other animals may have some level of ToM. A few – dolphins and certain apes – seem to have a very basic ability. But humans can go much further. Robin Dunbar and his colleagues have shown that we can have five – and sometimes six – levels of ToM, and they argue that we can do this because of the size of specific parts of our brain.

For example: you can guess (1) that your mother thinks (2) the teacher wants (3) the whole drama club to understand (4) the importance of turning up on time. When we think about fiction, it becomes even more complex: when you read a story, you know (1) that the author wants (2) you to believe (3) that the villain is desperate (4) to make his victim think (5) that he doesn't intend (6) to kill him.

The fact that we have brains that are big enough to do this allows us to have empathy. But just having a human brain is not enough. To develop the best possible empathy, we need several things including: skill, the opportunity to learn about other people, a developed brain, and stories.

Skill: Some people just seem to have better empathy than others – though it's possible that this extra empathy level was learnt during early childhood. On average, females tend to be better at this than males. (You can find references to male/female empathy in Resources.)

101

There are several possible reasons for this, most of which suggest that upbringing is the cause, not biology. It could be that young girls are more often praised for kindness, while boys are more often praised for being strong and brave. There may be an inborn brain difference which might allow females to develop this skill more easily than males, but the science on this is very unclear. Whatever the reason, we should aim to develop these skills equally in everyone.

Also, people on the autistic spectrum, including those with Asperger syndrome, usually find empathy difficult. However, many people with Asperger's work really hard to understand the behaviour of other individuals and sometimes learn these skills brilliantly.

Opportunities to learn about other people: If you've only met people who are a certain type, you may assume everyone is thinking similarly to you. For example, if your whole family is extrovert and confident, you may take a while to understand why some people are more reserved and need quiet time.

A developed brain: Empathy develops as our brains develop – look at my point about three- and four-year-olds. But empathy also seems to change during adolescence. I'll talk about that in a minute.

Stories: There's now a mass of evidence to suggest that stories, including true stories, help to develop empathy. Some scientists even argue that stories are *essential* to developing empathy. I disagree because I think that there are other ways to learn how people feel, such as by listening to them. But I do agree that stories are an incredibly powerful way to develop empathy.

EMPATHY OR SYMPATHY?

These words are often used as though they mean exactly the same thing. Actually, they don't, although they are very similar and both are just as important to friendship. I'll talk about both at the same time but you might like to know the exact difference.

Empathy is when you see a person's feelings from their point of view (as closely as that is possible) and you share something of their emotion and mental state. You properly feel something of the person's suffering and step as much as possible into their experience.

Sympathy doesn't go as far as that. Sympathy is when you react kindly to a person's suffering by trying to comfort them with words such as "I'm so sorry"; but you may not actually feel their pain. If you are empathetic you will probably also show sympathy, but you can be sympathetic even if you don't feel what the person is feeling.

One simple way to see the difference is this: you can have sympathy (or pity, which is a form of sympathy) for a bird with an injured leg, but you can't empathise because you can't really know or share what the bird is feeling. You know that if you had an injured leg you'd be feeling some pain and also fear and a desire to get help, but you've no idea if those things are part of a bird's pain. So, you can sympathise and show concern, but you're not empathising, or only on a shallow level at least.

Trying to be empathetic to a person is trying to understand properly and share the person's experience; trying to be sympathetic is offering support and solidarity, through friendship and human decency.

Both are good and both are equally relevant to friendship, which is why I'm talking about them together.

WHY DO STORIES HELP DEVELOP EMPATHY?

When we read or hear stories, we see into the mind of a character or characters in a particular situation, whether actual or made-up. We learn much more about the characters and their situation than we could if we just met and chatted to them. More than that, in fact: we can know more about the characters in a story than we know about our closest friend. Skilled writers, of both fictional and true stories, can give us that.

This allows us to do more than just understand or know how someone feels: it enables us to actually take on the feelings and experiences of that character. This is called "narrative transportation" – the state of mind when we actually start to feel like the character in some ways. We are "transported" into the mind of someone else.

This is what we do when we try to empathise with someone. We are not just trying to think how *we* would feel in their situation: we are trying to think how they actually do feel. That's very difficult and, to be honest, we can't know whether we've got it right, because no one can really know for certain what someone else is feeling. But empathy is the act of trying and at least partially succeeding.

So, if you or your friends are dealing with problems to do with divorce, stepfamilies, eating disorders, physical or mental illness, bereavement, abuse, alcohol, drugs, violence – the list is endless! – or if you just want to know what it might feel like to be in those situations, there will always be a story which shows people dealing with them.

Reading for pleasure – burying yourself in any book you enjoy – is a great way of becoming more empathetic towards others but also of boosting your own self-awareness and self-esteem. In short, it makes you wiser and stronger!

EMPATHY AND TEENAGE FRIENDSHIPS

The amount of empathy people have directly affects how they behave to other people. Of course, a few people seem to enjoy hurting others, but most people who say mean things don't actually think about or realize the effect. When someone makes a negative comment about your size, your hair, your voice, your face, your knobbly

SECTION THREE

knees – anything – they usually just haven't demonstrated empathy. They haven't put themselves in your shoes and asked themselves, "How would I feel if someone said that to me?"

Some teenagers naturally have more empathy than others and find it easier to understand what someone else is feeling. And because people who have less empathy are likely not to realize – or care – if they're hurting someone else, you'll find some of your friends and peers just don't realize what they're doing. They are perhaps less mature than you, less sensitive and aware.

Also, teenagers have not yet fully developed the brain areas that allow good empathy. The crucial brain area for this skill is the prefrontal cortex, which isn't properly developed until well into your twenties. Research shows that younger teenagers are least good at recognizing what someone is feeling based on looking at the expression in their eyes. (This is only one part of empathy, though.) That skill gradually increases as you move into adulthood. Even then, many people won't have fantastic empathy and never will.

Teenagers have so much else going on in their brains and lives that they often have to put themselves first, and don't think so sensitively about other people. Controlling feelings and behaviour takes brain-space, remember, as do stress, upset and worry. So it's not surprising if people behave in particularly unpleasant ways during the school years. I'm not making excuses, but I do think that understanding this is helpful for you and encourages you not to blame yourself. You'll sometimes hear people say that teenagers are less empathetic than older people. I don't believe this is necessarily true, but I do think there are aspects of adolescence, including brain changes, that make it harder.

THINGS TO THINK ABOUT

- Empathy is an advanced skill that grows during adolescence and isn't something many young teenagers have fully developed (though many still manage to be very sympathetic). This is no one's fault – not theirs or yours.

- Lots of adults have poor empathy skills, too. Sometimes, they just haven't developed them, and sometimes they have too much on their mind and no room left for thinking about other people. You may need to be very clear about how you feel, as the adults around you may not have worked it out themselves.

- As you read this book, your own empathy is inevitably growing. It's not fiction and it's not a story, but it's giving you powerful insight into how people's minds work and why they behave the way they do.

- Ask your school librarian about the possibility of

107

developing an empathy project, getting students to look at what they learn about other people from reading books. Think about characters in novels who have opened your eyes to someone else's life. (An organisation called EmpathyLab, mentioned in Resources, does this work in schools.)

QUIZ

How Empathetic are You?

This quiz tackles empathy and sympathy together. I've picked out things that can help you improve your friendships – although if you're empathetic but the people around you aren't, there's not too much you can do except find better friends!

Give yourself a score of 0, 1, 2, 3 or 4, depending on how strongly you agree with the following statements: 0 for "not at all", 4 for "extremely".

1. I believe it's important to listen really carefully and try to work out what people are feeling, because they might not feel the same as me about things.
2. I like the fact that people bring me their problems.
3. I never try to avoid listening to a friend's problems.
4. Even if I can't think of the right thing to say when a friend is going through a bad time, I still listen.
5. I tend to feel sympathy for someone who is suffering, even if I think it was their fault.
6. I enjoy reading about someone in a very different situation from my own because I like learning how other people might be thinking.

7. When I'm reading or watching a film, I often feel the same emotions as the characters and I think about them after the story or film is finished.
8. One of the things I like most about reading is that it helps me understand other people even better.
9. I think I'd be good in a job where I had to care for people.
10. I'm interested in other people and how we all think differently.
11. I notice other people's moods and will usually ask them how they are feeling.
12. If a friend is going through a bad time, I'll think about how to help them even when I'm not with them.
13. When I read about sad things in the news, I try to think about how I could help.
14. I've noticed that some people aren't good at understanding others. I am glad it's one of my skills.
15. I often take a long time choosing a present for someone because I'm thinking about whether they would like it, rather than whether I like it myself.

If you scored more than 40 out of 60, you are likely to have good levels of empathy. See if there are any specific questions where you could raise your score.

You'll notice that many of these questions aren't asking how *good* you are at being empathetic but how *important* it is to you. If you believe empathy is important, you will naturally want to take steps to become even better at it. You know that reading stories can help, but the great thing is that simply *trying* to be more empathetic will help you become just that. It's a skill and, like all skills, needs practice.

SECTION FOUR

Behaviour and Personality

When friendships go wrong or people are behaving in negative ways towards you, it's horrible. Social rejection activates similar brain regions to physical pain, so what you feel is very real and very unpleasant. You might be thinking it's your fault, that there's something about you that's "causing" their behaviour. But there are lots of reasons – nothing to do with you – that make people react as they do. It's reassuring and empowering to have an insight into some explanations for different human behaviour.

So, this section looks at all those explanations. Be aware that every behaviour may have a combination of different causes. You can't usually know for certain which one is responsible in any particular case. But they are all interesting to think about.

Everyone is changing

Your teenage years are a time of enormous change. Your body is changing and so is your brain, and there's lots going on at home and at school.

Your body – you are changing as you go through puberty. Sometimes that change is slow and sometimes it's fast. Developing too slowly or quickly can be difficult to manage. You might like the changes or you might not – and some people really don't. These changes can make you feel very self-conscious about your body. They can be positive and exciting, too, but they are definitely hard to ignore.

Your brain – huge changes happen in your brain from the age of around eleven to your mid-twenties. During adolescence you will both grow and lose connections between your brain cells; some areas of your brain will develop fast, while others are not fully developed. Remember that the last area to develop is your prefrontal cortex, the area which helps us control emotions, actions and decisions. This control – or lack of control – can make a big difference to friendships and relationships.

Your identity – as your body and mind go through such changes, you might be questioning things like the gender you were assigned at birth or your sexuality in terms of who you are physically attracted to. Your whole sense of who you feel you are and who you want to be can change, and it can be preoccupying, or confusing, or exciting, or a mixture of all three.

Your chemistry – whatever gender you are, you will experience increases in different hormones and these can cause mood swings of anger and sadness. If you or your friends are often snappy and moody, it will affect friendships.

Pressures and responsibilities – you are being pushed to consider your future and to take more responsibility for decisions and choices. You're told that these decisions will affect your future – it's a scary thought and the worry can make people behave in ways that seem selfish.

Schoolwork – everything is different compared with primary school. You're working for big exams; you have much more homework; you have to be at the right place at the right time, and there's less help for you in managing timetables and work.

Fears – when you were younger, adults could reassure you and protect you from the things you were scared of, whether it was thunderstorms or worry about getting a serious illness. They could say things like, "Don't worry, I'll always be here for you." But now they can't say that because you know that bad things happen that adults can't control. That's a massive change you're having to deal with, and for some it can cause big anxieties.

Family problems – if anything negative is going on in your family, such as illness or separation, you will probably

115

be far more aware of this than when you were younger. You may feel really preoccupied by it.

Friendships – these are changing in two ways: your friends are becoming different people, as you are, and as you get older you will be drawn to different friends because your interests will change.

So, everything is changing, in you and around you. While that's happening, it's little wonder that friendships can be under strain. Sometimes, you have enough to worry about in your own life and simply don't have time to look after your friends, or not all of them. Adults often accuse teenagers of being selfish, of being wrapped up in themselves. I'd say it's hardly surprising: there is so much for you to deal with and your first responsibility is to yourself.

THINGS TO THINK ABOUT

- Accept that things will change. Not just for you as a teenager but throughout life, people's needs change. Recognize that nothing stays the same for ever.
- Be prepared to let a friendship go if it isn't working.
- If someone no longer makes you feel comfortable, stop spending time with them. Of course, if the person is going through a hard

time and that's why they are behaving in a difficult way, be patient and sympathetic, as I mentioned when I was talking about managing friendships.

- Spend time with people who make you feel positive about yourself.
- Be open to new friendships and put yourself in situations where you can form new bonds. Join clubs and groups which share your interests.
- Try not to focus too much on "now" – your future life will be full of new opportunities when you go to college or start a job. If friendships are going wrong now, it's horrible, but it's only a snapshot moment of your life. There will be many better ones.
- Try to enjoy change. It's sad when good things come to an end, but that leaves room for new good things.
- Understand that the changes you're all going through are very powerful biological processes as well as social pressures. Overall, this is natural, universal and positive: you're becoming an adult, a new person, and you're only just starting to know what that new person needs. Be friends with yourself first and new friendships will follow.

117

Different personality types

We are all human. This means we have common experiences, feelings and behaviours. Our brains work generally in the same way. But there are also lots of differences between us, some small and some big. One of the range of differences comes from separate personality types.

We don't know exactly how personality develops, or exactly why we are the way we are, but we know that various factors make each person grow a particular set of personality "traits". It's a mysterious combination of your genes (which you inherit from your biological parents), upbringing (everything you learn and experience from parents or carers), environment (everything about your early home and school life), and all the things that happen to you from the moment of birth. It may even be that things that happened to you during or before birth also had an effect.

An interesting topic for discussion is whether the personality traits that you have now are "fixed" or whether they can change over time. I'm pretty sure they are not completely fixed: aspects can and will change, if you do certain things or if certain things happen. Your personality is part of who you are, but who you are can change in some ways. Sometimes that happens naturally, but I also believe that we can change some aspects of our personalities a little – or at least how our personalities make us react, if we want to and if we work really hard at it. Those are very big ifs!

I also think it's important to value who you are and to respect your own personality as just one way of being human. You don't have to change anything unless you want to. But if something about your personality is making you behave in a way that is preventing you achieving your goals and feeling good about yourself, you might decide to try to make some changes and adapt.

First, let's look at some personality traits, especially those that affect how people behave to each other. If you understand your friends and peers, and understand yourself, that gives you a great power over your life and experience. You can avoid a whole load of self-blame and unnecessary upset.

Remember, though: it's not only personality that makes people behave in particular ways. There are other things, which I'll cover later: peer pressure, stress and a whole load of situations that can be going on in people's lives.

PERSONALITY TYPES

Different psychologists have analysed us in different ways. Perhaps the most well-known way of categorising our behaviour is into the "big five" personality traits:

1. **Agreeableness** (pleasing people, thinking well of people, being easy-going)

2. **Conscientiousness** (being prepared and organised, finding it important to work hard and be serious)
3. **Neuroticism** (being a worrier with a tendency to be negative)
4. **Openness to experience** (enjoying new ideas and being open to art and the imagination)
5. **Extroversion** (needing to be with other people)

There has been such a huge amount of research into these five traits that many psychologists believe they're the most reliable way of describing our differences, particularly if you want to measure them and be scientific.

Others have suggested a sixth trait: honesty-humility. This is about how important fairness, honesty, modesty and generosity are to you. Whether you'd ever cheat – or how bad you'd feel if you did. If you score highly on honesty-humility, you'll be likely to treat others well and "do the right thing".

OTHER DIFFERENCES

Another whole set of differences involves our likes and the things we value. Psychologist Stephen Reiss calls these our "desires". How important are these things to you: order and tidiness, being independent, being a leader, learning new things, obedience to religion, people depending on you, status or fame, romance, physical activity, revenge, peacefulness? If you asked your friends to put them in order of importance, you'd get loads of different answers.

People have different reactions to stress, too. Some thrive on adrenalin; others hate the feeling of being stressed. Some people don't seem to get stressed at all, while others react to the smallest triggers. Some people push themselves to their absolute limit and others are satisfied with just getting by. I'll be talking about "Type A" and "Type B" personalities soon, and Type A people tend to be more stressed than the laid-back Type B people. (see page 132.)

We also differ in various other ways: easy-going or irritable, tolerant or intolerant, optimistic or pessimistic, sensitive or insensitive, positive or negative. The complete list would be a long one! I'm going to talk about the personality differences which most strongly affect your peers' behaviour towards you, and I'll show you inside the heads of the people around you. Inside your own head, too.

SECTION FOUR

INTROVERT OR EXTROVERT?

I find introversion and extroversion fascinating aspects of personality. Whichever end of the scale you feel you are, it can be incredibly empowering to understand the values of both.

Lots of people believe that introversion is about being shy and extroversion is about being a party animal. No, it's far more interesting and complex. It's really about energy levels and how our brains and bodies react biologically to the things around us, particularly to people and noise. Someone who is strongly extrovert gets a buzz out of being with people and gains energy from social situations, which is why they are often on top form at parties. But they also often enjoy peace and quiet, too, and many extroverts aren't noisy themselves. Someone who is more introverted *spends* energy in any social situation, whether it's a noisy party or a one-to-one chat with a good friend. That doesn't mean they can't do it or don't enjoy it – they can! – but it does mean they can be exhausted more quickly and may feel stressed if they don't get some peace. They *need* time on their own and that need tends to be greater in introverts.

No one is entirely extrovert or introvert: we are all somewhere on the scale and may also behave differently in different situations, or depending on how we feel. An introvert who happens to be feeling relaxed may find it easier to act more extrovertly. And natural extroverts sometimes behave in a more reserved way. But understanding the normal level of introversion/ extroversion of you and your friends gives you an important insight into behaviour. There's a quiz at the end of this section and you can find other tests and quizzes on the Internet. You'll also find a brilliant book and website listed in Resources.

Here are some of the common features of extroverts and introverts. Remember these are just tendencies, not rules.

Extroverts tend to:
- Focus outwards, looking for new experiences
- Find it easy to be outgoing
- Gain energy from social interaction
- Enjoy having lots of people around them – and need that
- Have a lot of super-positive emotions – desire, joy, excitement
- Enjoy new experiences, including risky ones; they may be thrill-seekers
- Not be self-conscious if they get something wrong in public
- Show their emotions clearly on their faces
- Enjoy working collaboratively

Introverts tend to:

- Focus inwards and particularly enjoy time spent thinking
- Be happy relaxing on their own and being quiet
- Be tired by social interaction, even when they are having a good time
- Prefer talking to one person at a time and enjoy focusing on one person or thing
- Have less "super-excited" emotions – prefer contentment to excitement
- Not be thrill-seekers or enjoy risk or thrill very much
- Suffer more from embarrassment
- Be more reserved about showing emotion
- Dislike working collaboratively; they often do their best work on their own

Both sets of people – as well as those who are right in the middle – are just as important. The world needs a mixture of personalities. Introverts are often judged negatively for being shy and not speaking up; extroverts are often judged negatively for being too loud and not thinking before they speak. But introverts bring valuable elements to a friendship: listening and thinking skills and sensitivity. Extroverts bring other important elements, such as energy and boldness. Both can make good and interesting things happen. Both need to understand and value each other more but most importantly, both need to understand what the other needs in order to feel good.

Because introverts become stressed if they do not have enough quiet time, they shouldn't be hassled to come out and be social all the time. And certainly shouldn't be made to feel boring or silly just because they want space. Extroverts can become bored and irritable if they don't have enough social activity, and they may be more prone to feeling lonely. Just ask your friends what they need and don't be afraid to say what you need.

If your friend is more extrovert than you, don't worry if they want to have lots of friends. Don't think they are "more popular" or that they are better in any way. You are both just different, with different strengths. Value each other equally. Be sensitive to your differences. And if sometimes your friend wants to spend time with someone else who can give them either the liveliness or the quiet that they need, don't take it personally.

CAN YOU BECOME MORE EXTROVERTED
IF YOU WANT TO?

Many introverts learn to perform as extroverts at least some of the time. I guess that's what I do. Many actors and comedians are, you may be surprised to know, introverts: they manage on stage because they have a role to play and don't have to reveal themselves so much. Most people get a buzz out of applause and public praise, so if you're an introvert who wants that, you'll need to overcome your introversion in order to get it.

Many of the things you have to do at school require you to perform like an extrovert: putting your hand up, presenting something to the class, making a speech, joining a club, attending the school dance or social engagements. All of those things bring advantages, including self-esteem, so it's definitely worth finding ways to do them.

Practice is the key. The more often you do a difficult or stressful action, the easier it is next time. Learning relaxation skills, discovering that the symptoms of nerves are only temporary, experiencing the positive feelings afterwards – all of these will help you. But another thing that can help is to tell someone else, either an adult or a friend, that you are suffering a bit from being an introvert and you need some support with the aspects you find hard.

Introverts may experience more embarrassment than extroverts and feel "awkward" and self-conscious. If this describes you, remind yourself that feeling awkward or embarrassed is perfectly common. They are positive emotions, designed to make you sensitive to others and to situations. Other people are usually not judging you nearly as much as you think, and lots of them will be really sympathetic to how you feel. Try to tell yourself that and then put it behind you. You could also learn some relaxation techniques (see Resources) to help how your body reacts to embarrassment.

So, I wouldn't suggest for one moment that you should try to stop being an introvert, but it is worth learning to do some of the things that an extrovert finds easier.

A final thought: don't assume that people who smile all the time and seem really happy actually are. Quiet people can be happy, too, and people who smile all the time can be hiding inner sadness or stress.

THINGS TO THINK ABOUT

- Can you think of any ways in which your introversion or extroversion may be hindering you? If so, do you want to ask anyone to help with some strategies? I think it would be great to discuss this with your teachers and to help them understand how you feel, too.
- If you're an introvert, realize that if you can be brave and face your fears, you will feel great about yourself *and* the next time it will be easier.
- If you're an extrovert, realize that although your energy and sparky company will often be hugely appreciated, sometimes you might seem

127

overwhelming to others. Occasionally extroverts attract the wrong sort of attention and may be told off more often because they are more noticeable.

- Understand and accept your own needs for noise or quietness, and understand that this is a biological response, not a deliberate one.
- Being introvert or extrovert is not the only thing that determines who you are. Everything else I talk about in this book mixes together to create each individual's make-up.

QUIZ

Are you more introvert or more extrovert?

Remembering that people are usually somewhere between very introvert and very extrovert, and remembering that your answers to these questions may change depending on how you are feeling and what's going on in your life, here's a simple quiz to give you some idea of where you might fall on the scale.

Give yourself a score of 0, 1, 2, 3 or 4, depending on how strongly you agree with the following statements: 0 for "not at all", 4 for "extremely".

1. When you've been doing something with friends and it's time to go home, you want the social situation to go on for longer.
2. If a trip to the cinema with friends were cancelled, you would be very disappointed and try to organise something else.
3. If there's a minor conflict or disagreement amongst your friends, you find it quite easy to deal with this.
4. You feel excited and full of energy when you've been chatting to people.

5. If a school trip is coming up, with a couple of nights away, you would really be looking forward to this.

6. You think a holiday would be totally boring if it consisted of reading, lying in the sun and doing nothing, with very few (or maybe even no) people your own age.

7. You usually prefer a joint project or piece of work, rather than working on something by yourself.

8. If you're choosing a physical activity, you usually like team games/activities (such as football, basketball) more than solo ones (such as yoga, swimming).

9. You enjoy situations where you have to think quickly and make decisions without having lots of time to plan.

10. You feel confident about taking a leadership role and telling people what they need to do.

11. You are fairly comfortable giving a talk or presentation to your class, even though you might feel a little bit nervous just before.

12. If there's something you want to say in a group setting, you can do this without getting anxious or worrying about what to say.

13. In group settings, you often entertain everyone with your jokes or stories, or just by being lively.

14. You don't really like being on your own, or at least not for long. You need people and activity around you.

15. If you get an answer wrong or make a small mistake in front of your friends, you're not that bothered. You don't let it get to you.

Add up your scores. A higher score (out of a maximum 60) indicates more extroversion and a lower score reveals more introversion. But even if you score significantly as one or the other, you will probably find that there were one or two questions where you were strongly in the other direction. Those answers can give you a clearer picture of what you need in terms of interaction with other people. For example, you might be strongly introvert, needing plenty of quiet time, but still enjoy doing collaborative work or be a confident leader or public speaker.

Type A or B?

The idea that people could be divided into "Type A" and "Type B" began in the 1950s with two heart specialists, Ray Rosenman and Meyer Friedman. They noticed that heart attacks seemed more common in people with a certain set of personality traits. They called these Type A people. (Don't worry: we now know that heart attacks and heart disease happen for many other reasons, and you can be a perfectly healthy Type A person.)

What are the behaviours? As with other personality types, you will find that people won't be completely one thing or another but will fall somewhere along a scale.

Type A people tend to:
- Be ambitious and set themselves very high targets
- Need to win – coming second may not be enough
- Be easily irritated and angered
- Be impatient about delays – always rushing into things
- Be anxious about something a long time before it's going to happen

- Have difficulty sleeping
- Find it hard to "let go" of things that have gone wrong
- Be competitive – or avoid competition because they are afraid of not winning
- Work too hard – and may become ill because of it
- Enjoy being busy and feel bored when they don't have lots to do
- Try to do several things at once
- Be frustrated by Type B behaviours

Type B people tend to:
- Set achievable targets
- Be more easily satisfied with what they've achieved
- Be more interested in enjoying a game or an activity than in winning
- Underachieve because they didn't practise early enough or for long enough
- Not worry about things far in advance
- Have less difficulty in sleeping

133

- Not worry so much when they make a mistake or don't do very well
- Be laid-back, relaxed, unfazed and unflappable
- Find it easy to switch off at weekends and on holiday
- Be good at prioritising and focusing on one thing at a time
- Find it hard to understand the behaviours of Type A people

It is very hard – probably impossible – to change this aspect of your nature. However, it helps to know where you fit on the Type A/B scale, because there are times when you might want or need to try to adapt your behaviour. For example, coming up to exams, a Type A person needs to make an effort to build relaxation into each day and Type B people may need to get cracking earlier than their laid-back natures wish.

Also, understanding the A/B aspects of the people around you helps explain why your friends and peers behave as they do. Then you can accept that this is how they are – two different types of person with two different sets of motivations. If a Type B rolls her eyes and tells you to chill or a Type A is annoyed by your calmness, don't blame yourself: put it down to personalities.

Be cautious, however: you can't be completely sure someone is Type A or Type B because you don't know what's in their head. For example, although being competitive is a Type A trait, a Type A person can also be so secretly afraid of failure that they won't compete at all. So, if your friend always opts out of competitive sport or games, don't assume they aren't competitive: they may just not want to risk losing.

THINGS TO THINK ABOUT

- If you are a Type A personality, recognize that you may be more vulnerable to stress. Notice when you are setting yourself impossible targets. Perhaps you could reward yourself more often and learn relaxation techniques that you can use when necessary.

- If you are a Type B personality, recognize that you may get behind with your work through delaying or simply not getting nervous enough. Think ahead to what you want to achieve and remember that, for most people, hard work rather than luck is what leads to success. How will you feel if you don't get your act together in time?

QUIZ

Type A or Type B?

This quiz gives you a sense of whether you tend to behave more as a Type A or Type B. Remember: tests like this only give an indication of how you tend to behave and react. The results can depend on who you're measuring yourself against. For example, if the people you spend most time with happen to be strongly A or B, you might find that you subconsciously compare yourself with them and your answers may be affected.

Give yourself a score of 0, 1, 2, 3 or 4, depending on how strongly you agree with the following statements: 0 for "not at all", 4 for "extremely".

1. I am very competitive – if I'm involved in something, I really need to win. Coming second would annoy me because I'd feel I could have done better.
2. I tend to eat and drink more quickly than most people – I often hardly notice what I'm tasting because I eat it without thinking.
3. I often take on too much and then worry that I won't be able to complete everything on time and well enough.
4. I tend to become irritable if other people mess around

and don't take things seriously.

5. I find it hard to allow myself relaxation time – exams and work are too important, and I always want to get those done first.

6. Even when it is time to relax, like a weekend or holiday, I find myself always wanting to do something.

7. Sometimes I avoid joining in a new activity because I might not be very good at it.

8. When I make a mistake, I find it very difficult to let it go.

9. I would not call myself laid-back and easy-going!

10. If I'm passed over for a prize or position that I feel I deserve, I find it very hard to get over it.

11. When someone gives me constructive criticism, I find it hard to use it positively because I get too cross with myself for not getting it right the first time.

12. If I have a deadline for a task, I always start it early, rather than waiting till nearer the time.

13. It's important for me to be organised – disorganisation and mess make me tense.

14. If I'm going for a walk, I want a target and I want to get there fast. Ambling along listening to birdsong is not my idea of a walk!

15. I always set myself impressive goals and targets that most people would consider extremely demanding.

A score higher than 40 out of 60 suggests that you are more of a Type A personality. But you should also notice whether you've scored high on certain questions and low on others, because you might have some but not all the Type A traits. It's possible, for example, that although you are competitive, often in a hurry and setting yourself high standards, you still find it easy to relax.

If you want to get a clearer idea, with more detailed questions, look for some of the free online tests.

Neurotic or laid-back?

Neurotic literally means "nervous" or "reacting to nerves". It generally refers to overreaction, rather than something wholly positive. Reacting to real threat with a nervous response is healthy and normal: it helps us avoid danger and act super quickly to get ourselves out of trouble. But some people are more reactive to danger and anxiety than others, and we say that such people are more "neurotic".

Certainly, being neurotic doesn't feel great. It can spoil your enjoyment of life and make you spend far too long worrying about things you can't control. The reason it's relevant to friendships is that you are more likely to spend a lot of time fretting about what you've said, what someone else has said, what everyone thinks and what might happen.

Also, people who are highly neurotic can be quite tiring to live with! They need extra attention and empathy. And that's what this chapter will give you: understanding of yourself and of others if you or they – or both – have a tendency to be neurotic.

Let's look at what highly neurotic people are like. They tend to:

- Be anxious, worried and afraid
- Be envious or jealous
- Be very superstitious

139

- Check things often – and then still worry that they haven't checked properly
- Overreact to quite small threats
- Overthink
- Never think they've done enough
- Worry what people think of them or about something they've said
- Imagine dramatically bad things happening – "What if...?"
- Be more vulnerable to mental illnesses such as depression, anxiety disorders, phobias
- Be more likely to suffer from panic attacks (This is when you become completely overwhelmed by terrible fear and a racing heart, and you may even think you're going to die – which you are not.)
- Have intrusive negative thoughts – repeated unpleasant thoughts that go round and round in your head and are hard to ignore

WHAT CAN YOU DO IF YOU OR ANY OF YOUR FRIENDS OR PEERS ARE LIKE THIS?

Having some neurotic tendencies is very common and almost everyone will recognize at least a few of those experiences. So, don't regard it as an illness: it's just hypersensitivity to threat. Be sympathetic towards the neurotic person – including yourself. Understand that the feelings may not be pleasant but can be managed and can improve as you get older or if you get help such as counselling. Sometimes a neurotic friend may be too wrapped up in dealing with their own anxiety to be kind to you. Just recognizing this will help you not blame yourself. But it's also OK to tell them if they aren't being kind to you; you can tell them that you understand that they have their own worries but that they should realize that they are accidentally hurting you, for example.

Next, recognize that sometimes neuroticism can tip into a level of distress that needs expert help such as counselling. If your feelings of anxiety are overwhelming, constant or very frequent, that's not something you should have to deal with on your own. Anyone suffering depression, serious anxiety, repeated panic attacks or any degree of neuroticism that is spoiling their daily life should feel able to ask for medical advice. If this applies to you, talk to someone. You can start with any trusted adult and they will guide you.

Finally, understand that, although neuroticism is a natural personality trait and can't be simply "cured", there are lots of ways to make it feel better and to stop it controlling your life; you can learn to manage how you react to anxiety. You'll find some suggestions below.

THINGS TO THINK ABOUT

- A worry is only a thought and a thought is only

a pathway in your brain, which you created by having the thought. The more times you have the thought, the stronger the pathway becomes. But you can replace it with a better thought, and the more times you have that one, the stronger the better pathway will become. So, each time your worry pops into your head, make yourself think of a positive thing instead. It's hard at first but gets easier.

- Sharing anxieties with a friend can be really helpful. You will often find that your friends have many of the same worries. They will also have some different ones, and by talking you can help both yourself and others.

- If you're going round thinking that your dark thoughts and worries are "weird", don't: whatever your worry, there's someone out there thinking the same.

- As you grow older, you will learn different ways to control your worries. Sometimes you'll learn through your own experience of life; or from reading books; and sometimes you might need to talk to someone with a professional counselling skill.

- You may notice that if one worry comes into your mind, it often triggers more worries – and the worries become like a snowball, going round and round and getting bigger. So, when this happens, say to yourself, "Ah, here comes that worry cycle – I can head it off by choosing to do something fun, positive, energetic."

QUIZ

Are you too anxious?

This set of questions is designed to reveal whether you may be too anxious for your own good and your neurotic trait may be dominating your life. As with all the quizzes in this book, remember that your mood and what's going on in your life at the time you do it will affect how you answer.

Give yourself a score of 0, 1, 2, 3 or 4, depending on how strongly you agree with the following statements: 0 for "not at all", 4 for "extremely".

1. I seem to be more anxious than most of the people I know well.
2. I spend a lot of time worrying about bad things that might happen but that I know probably won't.
3. When I'm worrying about something that might happen, I construct whole stories and scenarios in my head, and I can get quite carried away by my imagination.
4. If someone mentions something frightening or there's a bad thing on the news, I can feel my heart race immediately and I might feel a bit dizzy.
5. I have had more than two panic attacks.

6. When I'm nervous about something – like an exam – the worry stops me being able to work well.
7. I am often extremely jealous of other people and wonder why I can't be like them. This feeling can dominate my thoughts.
8. I tend to expect the worst.
9. I tend to worry about something a very long time in advance and will have many sleepless nights long before it's actually time to prepare.
10. I have a habit of continually checking that my phone is with me – I'll pat my pocket, even though I know it's there.
11. If someone around me is ill, I take active steps to avoid catching the germs: I turn away, hold my breath, avoid touching things, wash my hands a lot, and generally feel anxious.
12. I'm very superstitious. For example, if last time I wore certain shoes something terrible happened, I'd worry a bad thing would happen if I wore them again.
13. My anxiety is triggered by any mention of certain negative words. When I hear these words, I'm likely to have repeated negative thoughts over the next hours or days.
14. I know that being anxious sometimes is a normal emotion, but my anxiety often stops me from doing some things that I want to do.
15. I am feeling much more anxious after answering these questions!

If you answered 4 to question 15, I am sorry! If you scored more than 45 on this test, that suggests quite a high level of anxiety or neurotic tendencies, which may be spoiling your enjoyment of life and affecting your wellbeing. But there are some things you can do to help yourself. I have a lot of stress management advice on my website (see Resources) but here are a few tips to start with:

1. Recognize that a high score does not mean that you have an illness but it does mean that you need to look after yourself and your stress levels.

2. When you find yourself thinking about one of the things that makes you anxious, practise a diversion technique: either do or think about something that makes you feel good, whether it's reading an engrossing book, daydreaming about a desert island, writing a poem or colouring in – anything that helps you escape from your worries for a while.

3. Practise a breathing or meditation technique (see Resources).

Nasty people

There are some characteristics which are very antisocial, entirely selfish and which damage both individuals and the communities they live in. People with these personality traits are difficult to be friends with, and they *can* be dangerous to know. These traits are sometimes called "the dark triad": scheming, narcissism and psychopathy.

Many people have small elements of these traits in them – we all have faults. If you find that you have aspects of these things in your personality, it's good to be aware of them: knowing yourself allows you to have better control over negative impulses. It can sometimes explain why you might fall out with your friends. It's also possible that you don't *really* have these traits but you *appear* to, so people judge you as if you have. Perhaps, for example, your self-consciousness makes you say the wrong thing or not notice you have upset someone. If you realize this, it gives you the chance to correct that false impression.

You may well recognize some of these behaviours in the people you don't like at school. If you understand why they do what they do, it can help you keep them at arm's length. And that's the best thing to do: stay out of their way. You'll meet such characters at various times in your life, and when you recognize the type, staying away will be easier.

SCHEMERS

This type of person is sometimes called Machiavellian, after the fifteenth-century Italian writer Niccolò Machiavelli, who described why in his view rulers have to do cruel things in order to rule effectively. So, "Machiavellian" refers to people who will selfishly scheme and do anything – including hurting others – to get what they want. They might say, "The end justifies the means" – in other words, it's fine if someone is hurt in order for them to achieve their goal. Sometimes they don't even know they are doing it.

Suppose you are really keen to get into the football team. There are several ways of going about it. (Only one of them is my advice!)

1. Practise really hard; turn up to all training sessions; show the coach how hard-working you are; and become good enough for the team.
2. Practise hard but also be really nice to the coach in the hope that you are picked over someone else equally good.
3. If there's someone better than you whose place in the team threatens yours, do something to jeopardise that person's chances: get them into trouble, focus the coach's attention on their mistakes, trip them up.

Obviously, the last one is wrong. It is Machiavellian. Anyone who would do this is not someone you can trust.

But... If someone you know behaved like this, it's

possible it was a one-off, or they were going through a really bad patch which led to a distorted sense of right and wrong, and a lack of control and decency. So, perhaps they aren't Machiavellian by nature, but it was Machiavellian behaviour.

Also, although being deceitful in order to prevent someone joining the team is obviously wrong, there are shades of grey. For example, what if you were supposed to tell the other player there was an extra practice that evening and you didn't? That's not good. But what if the reason was that you didn't see them in time? Depends on how hard you tried. Maybe there was a choice between spending time searching for the other player or getting to your own music lesson on time. Machiavellian? Not so much.

Lots of people have a slight Machiavellian side to them, or can find themselves in a situation where they do something a bit unpleasant or dishonest to get what they want. Psychologists have shown that most people would do harm to others in certain situations (see Resources). Perhaps someone is afraid or lacks confidence, so they are persuaded to steal or to join in bullying or risky behaviour. It's not nice but it's a human trait that it's best to be on the lookout for, in yourself and in others.

If you make a mistake and do something you feel was wrong, try to forgive yourself and avoid doing it again. Everyone makes mistakes; everyone can lose their good judgement when under strain. Learn from it, apologize if relevant and move on.

NARCISSISTS

In ancient Greek mythology, Narcissus was a young man who was incredibly gorgeous – and he knew it! He was vain and self-absorbed. To punish him, the goddess Nemesis lured him to a pool where he saw a reflection of himself and fell in love with it. The story goes that he ended up killing himself because he realized that his reflection couldn't love him back. So, narcissism has come to mean "loving yourself too much".

On the other hand, we are often told we need to love ourselves. Self-esteem is part of that, surely? But narcissists are too wrapped up in themselves, and put themselves before others in a way that can destroy relationships and harm the people around them.

Narcissists can be difficult to be friends with because they find it hard to deal with other people being more beautiful, clever, sporty, popular, etc. It's all about them. At first they can be fun to be with, but as soon as things don't go their way, they can become very difficult indeed.

As with any other trait, this is not something people choose to have. Narcissism can have its roots in a troubled or neglected early childhood, so don't be too hard on people with this personality type.

PSYCHOPATHS

I hope you don't know any psychopaths but you still might be interested in knowing about them! The literal meaning of the word psychopath is "sick personality". We tend to mean anyone who seems to care so little about other people's feelings that they would commit crimes against others without feeling sorry afterwards. They have no conscience or sense of guilt. Sometimes people use the word "sociopath" instead, especially for someone who does have a conscience but isn't very influenced by it.

At its extreme, psychopathy can be a mental disorder and then it is called "antisocial personality disorder". It can be something a person is born with (in which case it may be inherited) or it can develop from a damaged childhood or experiences that mean a person's normal emotions aren't properly switched on.

What is a psychopath like? Often, you won't know someone is a psychopath until they behave in a very extreme way, as they are very good at deceiving people. Conmen are often psychopaths. (And, statistically, more men than women fall into this personality category.) They don't seem to feel or recognize responsibility. Things are always someone else's fault – this also applies to narcissists. Psychopaths are dangerous because they don't have the moral boundaries or work to the same rules as other people. They tend to use violence more easily and without thought for the effect on anyone else. They are often extremely over-confident about their abilities.

Again, these behaviours can appear in lots of people who are not psychopaths. There are many other reasons for someone being impulsive or having anger-management issues, and when people are going through major stress they can act in these ways. So, don't be too quick to assume that someone is a psychopath: it's quite rare.

THINGS TO THINK ABOUT

- Has anything I've said in this section so far helped explain any of the negative behaviours going on around you? Has this made you feel better about how people react to you?
- Perhaps you have gained insight into yourself, too. It probably makes you feel better to realize that some of your reactions and emotions are not your "fault", but still may be things you could change a bit if you wanted to. Remember, it's not about altering your personality, but just changing some reactions and behaviours that you feel would help you.
- Do you prefer to be friends with people who are very similar to you or do you feel it's also fun to be friends with people who have different characteristics? Do your friends tend to be the same or very different?

- Can you see the same personality differences in the adults around you? Do you think you've inherited traits from your biological parents or been more affected by your environment and early childhood?
- If you have brothers and sisters, can you see ways in which you're the same and ways in which you're different?
- Do you think you know some people who fit the "dark triad" of schemers, narcissists or psychopaths? If so, be cautious: you may be wrong and they may have different, more temporary reasons for their negative behaviour. But I recommend you avoid relationships with anyone who behaves in these ways. And don't try to fight or annoy them. Walk away.
- If you are in a friendship with someone whose narcissism, scheming or lack of empathy is hurting you, you can say, "Your behaviour is hurting me." But you can also say nothing and withdraw from the friendship. What I don't think you should do is put up with them making you feel bad. Very narcissistic people are difficult to live with and will tend to keep making you feel bad. You don't deserve that. Better that they learn that this behaviour is not going to get them friends.

- Don't think you'll be able to change someone who has the dark traits I've described in the last chapter. Maybe one day they will become a better person, but you don't deserve to be damaged along the way. Move on to something better.

Family position

Where a person is in their family can make a difference to how they feel about themselves, their self-esteem and confidence. So it can also affect behaviour. Whether someone is an only child, the eldest of two or three, the eldest of many, the second or third, or "baby" of the family: all these things can influence how that person reacts to other people. Also, we each learn certain skills during our childhood: how to survive, how to get the things we need, how to get on with other people. Our position in the family is one of the factors we've learnt to deal with, often without noticing.

There are good and bad things about every family position, but in this book I'm really focusing on possible negatives, because those are what can get in the way of friendships. And I talk about "children" because it's in the early childhood years that the behaviour patterns I mention above are formed. By the time you're teenagers, patterns are quite deeply set.

Of course, many people don't fit these generalisations at all. There are so many other factors to consider than whether you have a younger or older brother or sister, or three. But your early childhood will make a difference to how you are now, and interaction with siblings – or not having siblings – is a major part of early childhood. How your parents managed the relationships between you all in your earliest years makes a huge difference, too – and it's not always easy for parents to get it right. They might accidentally say the wrong thing, perhaps leading to a sister being jealous of a brother, or the other way round. Or they may underestimate the difficulties posed by stepfamily relationships. Parents do make mistakes – and sometimes a lot of mistakes! Here are some ideas about how different positions in the family *might* negatively influence behaviour.

Single children might find it hard to fit in with peers, because they are sometimes more used to talking to adults than to other children. This means they can develop quite "adult" ways of talking that make them seem different from other children. Of course, if a single child has had lots of opportunities to play with other children – perhaps with cousins or at nursery – these effects are less likely.

A single child is very often the centre of their parents' world, with no competition from siblings, so they might act more selfishly and find it harder to cooperate. They often like being on their own and can sometimes *seem* "aloof" or shy. Also, because of that extra attention from parents, they often know more than other children.

An older child, with just one younger sibling is often used to being "the best", because they will have been ahead of their younger sibling in everything. Although this can give them confidence, they might equally have insecurity because they feel the need for status, and when that is threatened they find it difficult.

The age gap will make some difference, too. If it's less than about two years, this can be hard for the older child because their parents suddenly had to switch attention to a new baby while the first was still very young. So, although older children have the advantage of being the first to do things and usually feel superior to a younger sibling, they can also be jealous of the younger one's attention. This might make them a bit insecure in their friendships.

An oldest child with two or more younger siblings is often in a similar situation to the above, but a lot of difference can be made by the age gaps. If the younger siblings are close in age, the oldest might be left out and feel jealous and insecure. A group of three is often tricky, and any one of them can feel left out.

A younger child of two may struggle to keep up, always feeling second best; they often see the older sibling learning new skills and being praised by parents. The younger child may also be overprotected and end up being more fragile (though this same protection may equally give them confidence and security). Younger children can turn out to be very bold and determined – after all, they've seen the older one make things look easy.

157

Or they can end up lacking in confidence because they were always lagging behind.

A youngest of three or more is often very independent and enjoys being different. By the time a third child comes along, the parents will probably be more confident, and certainly more experienced, than they were with the first two. And the older children might have been able to help, too. The youngest child often doesn't expect lots of attention because they're used to not getting it! They're used to being in large groups, including different ages, so they may have extrovert tendencies. Being independently minded can make them stubborn and possibly even insensitive to others' needs. They don't always crave praise or attention, so they may not appreciate those who do.

A middle child is often regarded as being in a difficult position. He or she has a good chance of feeling insecure because of having an older sibling achieving things and growing up faster, and a younger sibling getting all the attention as the baby. Middle children often work hard to please other people, which can make them more vulnerable to criticism or nasty words.

What about gender? Surely whether siblings are brothers or sisters can make a difference? Yes, it can, in lots of complicated ways, big or small. For a start, boys and girls are often treated differently, even when parents try to be completely unbiased and fair. But remember that "boy" and "girl" are not two completely separate things. How each person identifies and expresses their gender will be individual, leading to infinite combinations of sibling interactions. You might see a "sister" or a "brother" but what you really have is a sibling whose gender identity, whether binary or fluid, is one part of who they are. And that will affect you in often unpredictable ways.

What you can't do is work out how your life would be different if you had siblings of different genders from the ones you have. After all, despite the advertisements aimed at one gender or another, not all people fit the stereotypes of how boys or girls, or men or women, behave. We are more complicated than that.

So, it will often make a difference whether your siblings are brothers or sisters but often it won't; and usually you won't be able to say exactly how.

What about stepfamilies? Stepbrothers and stepsisters create a whole other set of complicated possibilities. I won't go into detail, because this book will end up being far too long, but I will state the obvious: the complications of stepfamilies are immense and can have huge effects on emotions and behaviour. After all, both sets of children or teenagers have so far spent their whole lives in one family position and suddenly it changes for everyone. It can take

159

time to settle into a "new normal" and the relationships will continue to change, for better or worse, over the years.

THINGS TO THINK ABOUT

- Is there anything about your position in the family that you think affects how you behave and feel, and the sort of person you are?
- If you're trying to work out why someone is behaving in a particular way, is there something about their family position that may be influencing them? Might they be insecure? How they feel in their family will usually spill over into their friendships, too, because it has an effect on how they behave.

Other people's lives

There is more to our lives than our personalities. Things that happen to us and around us are important, too. As a teenager, you may have a whole load of different things going on in your life, influencing how you feel. And how we feel alters how we behave, remember. If you're angry, sad or worried, it's really hard to behave perfectly towards the people around you. You might be snappy or say things you don't mean, or perhaps meant at that moment but wish you hadn't said. It's harder to focus on what someone else is feeling when you're preoccupied with your own worries. And at really difficult times of our lives, we often don't behave in ways we feel proud of.

I've looked at how you're all changing and at personality differences, but now I want to talk about other things that could be going on in the life of someone you're having problems with, whether it's a friend or an ex-friend or someone who isn't a friend at all.

Psychologists talk about "preoccupation", the idea that part of the brain can be "preoccupied" by something and therefore has less room for other important actions. This is because all thoughts, including worries, occupy brain "bandwidth", leaving you with less capacity to do difficult things. And difficult things include thinking of something nice to say when you feel the opposite of nice! People are more likely to be bad-tempered when they are stressed or too busy. So, in order to have good control over our words and actions, we need not to be too preoccupied: our brain needs not to be too busy.

Here are some suggestions of things that might be going on in the minds of people around you (or in your own mind). There are loads more possibilities, but I hope this will give you an idea of just what a massive range of things can affect people's behaviour towards you.

Emotional things:
- A family money situation
- Worry about parents splitting up
- A stressful stepfamily situation – could be a new partner, or any number of really annoying or worrying or upsetting situations
- A major relationship issue to deal with – splitting up, wanting to split up, not wanting to split up
- A close friend or relative being very ill
- Someone saying something mean
- Feeling self-conscious about weight
- Being pressured to have sex by a boyfriend or girlfriend and worrying about this
- Anxiety about exams

- Not being picked for the team/play/performance and feeling undermined by that
- Feeling bored with school. Perhaps feeling irritated by people who seem to manage school without difficulty
- Parents piling on the pressure and not understanding the effect on emotion
- A parent suffering from depression
- Self-harming and the emotions surrounding that

Physical things:
- Headaches or stomach aches, which are common in adolescence and very often tied up with stress, make it hard to concentrate or behave nicely
- Exhaustion – loads of sleepless nights and too much work
- Feeling rubbish, with no energy

- A "chronic" medical condition such as asthma or eczema or irritable bowel syndrome (NB: "chronic" doesn't mean "serious" – it means "lasting a long time")
- Dyslexia or dyspraxia, which are common disabilities, can make people lose self-esteem
- Not eating properly, affecting mood and energy
- Severe period pains or any other pain

THE PAST

What happens to you when you are very young has a big effect on the kind of person you become. If bad things happen in early childhood, it can have a negative impact on things such as self-esteem, trust and confidence. There's something called "attachment theory", which looks at what can happen if a baby and small child can't build a strong set of bonds with a loving adult carer. It doesn't matter whether it's a mother or father, and it doesn't have to be a biological parent, but the love has to be consistent and strong, with enough attention given to the baby ensuring it has everything it needs: food, warmth, protection, eye contact and smiles. There are lots of reasons why this sometimes doesn't happen.

Why am I telling you this? Because someone who behaves in a way that's hostile, aggressive and unfriendly, or very changeable and unpredictable, just might be like this because they had a really tough early childhood. And that, of course, is not their fault. I think it's right to feel sorry for people who have been damaged by negative things in their childhood, even if that damage affects others.

However, if someone is like that, you should not have to suffer and it's not your responsibility to try to change them. Of course, if it's one of your friends, you'll want to try and show them that you do love them, and perhaps they will learn to accept that friendship. But it's not easy being friends with someone who is often hostile or hurtful. If your friend is suffering the effects of a really difficult childhood, that's the sort of thing that professional counselling can help with because this damage does not have to be permanent. But the person has to want help and the help has to be professional.

Also, although the person being mean to you may be doing so for the reasons I've mentioned, you can't be sure. So, it would be wrong to make that judgement. Just consider that it's a possible reason.

JUST FEELING DOWN

We all have better days and worse days – and weeks and months, and sometimes even whole terms or years. Times when we behave less well than others and make more mistakes. My worst year was the second to last year at school. My school reports at the end of that year were very critical about my behaviour. But one teacher said she thought I was unhappy. Well spotted, that teacher! I was a worried, pressured, introverted teenager who didn't feel that she fitted in.

When people are feeling negative about themselves, or have things preoccupying them, it often comes out as mean or negative behaviour towards others. I'm not making excuses but trying to give an explanation and make you realize that how people behave towards you is usually them, not you.

THINGS TO THINK ABOUT

- Remember that you, too, will often behave less well when you're worried, upset, ill, tired or stressed. Try to recognize when that is happening and take time to do something relaxing to calm yourself and improve your wellbeing.
- If someone is behaving badly, you'll need to work out whether the right thing is to walk away or to call them out on it and tell them it's unacceptable. And the decision will completely depend on the situation. Before you say anything, though, ask yourself whether it will benefit you.
- If a friend seems to be in a bad mood and snaps at you, you could try asking them if they're OK,

rather than reacting angrily. If you can find out (without nagging!) whether something is making them feel irritable, you will probably discover they are grateful and they might even apologize for snapping. If you are just angry back, it will probably start an argument, so you need to work out if that is going to help or not.

- All of these things apply to adults, too. So, next time your parents or teachers seem extra irritable, you'll probably find there's a reason for it that has nothing to do with you!

Peer pressure and group behaviour

Peer pressure and group behaviour can cause various problems. Perhaps you want to be in a group (or you were in one) and they are excluding you. Or you are in the group but are worried, because they are making you do things you don't want to do. Perhaps you aren't in the group but you can see them treating someone else badly. Or you have no wish to be in the group, but their behaviour is affecting you because they are picking on you. Sometimes a whole year group can be affected by the actions of a few "leaders". In that case, it can be difficult for students who actually want to work hard to be brave enough to ignore pressure from the others.

Adults sometimes imply that only teenagers react to peer pressure and display group behaviour. They ask, "Why do teenagers follow their friends' influence, even when they know it's the wrong thing to do?"

Adults are wrong to identify this as a *teenage* behaviour. Adults react to peer pressure, too. We humans have evolved to copy the people around us to an extent, in order to fit in and build bonds and connections. People even unconsciously imitate facial expressions and movements. Adapting to the behaviour of the people around you – whatever age you are – is healthy and positive because, as you now know, we have a deep need for social groups, going back many thousands of years to when early humans found that groups were essential for survival: finding food, looking after young, offering protection, hunting, passing on information. Even if you don't like large groups, you still want to know that you have people you can turn to, be relaxed with, and who won't exclude you.

So, adults are wrong to think of peer pressure as being especially a teenage thing. It's human social behaviour. But there's an extra element to being a teenager that makes peer pressure even more important: teenagers are on a journey from the protection of their first group – their family – towards independence. As you move away from spending all your time with your family group, you need to make new groups – new "families". But all those other friends and groups are changing, too. You have to work hard to be accepted by a group, and when you're in a group you often feel you need to do certain things to be accepted. You are trying to strengthen the new bonds.

Groups often share tastes, and following certain fashions or trends is one way you gel with your group. This is quite subconscious and natural. For example, you might start liking the same bands as your friends, supporting the same football team, or wearing a particular style of clothes or doing your hair in a certain way. You're not being shallow and changing your tastes deliberately, or pretending to like something for the sake of fitting in. You will often find that you actually do like what your

169

group likes. Your tastes can change in order to conform.

But maybe you're a genuine "non-conformist", who refuses to go along with a group behaviour and has their own very individual style. You may enjoy pushing the boundaries a bit and being noticed for being original. In that case, you might be drawn towards other non-conformists and develop strong friendships with some of them. In a way, they then become your invisible "group", even if groups aren't your thing. They can still be there for support and they can also still be an influence on you.

One thing I remind adults is that as teenagers you can afford to reject or be rude to your adults because you know (or should know) that they will not desert you, but you can't always rely on your friends not deserting you. You're still building those friendships and they are fragile. Sometimes, you feel you have to do things to be part of the group, even if you know, deep down, that those things aren't right or sensible.

They can be good friends, those groups, helping you develop your new, independent identity; but they can create pressure, too. Sometimes you might go along with that pressure because it can be difficult if you don't: being shunned by your "group" is really tough and can cause sadness, anxiety and dark thoughts. I mentioned at the start of Section Four that this activates the same brain pathways as physical pain does. In fact, at the extreme, or if it goes on too long, being isolated can contribute to depression and mental illness. We really do need friends, for our mental health.

That's why I believe teenagers so often seem to care more about what their friends and peers think than what their parents and carers think. You can't afford not to. It's hardwired into us all and can be very difficult to resist.

RISK-TAKING AND PEER PRESSURE

The teenage brain seems to reflect all of this, too. Imagine for a moment a risk-taking situation. Imagine you're with your group and someone suggests doing something exciting but wrong or risky. If you stopped to think, you'd be able to give reasons why you shouldn't do it. But other networks in your brain – the "reward system" areas – are flooded with a chemical called dopamine. If we could scan your brain, we'd see lots of activity in the areas relating to thrill-seeking and excitement. But research predicts that there'd be more activity in those areas when you're with your friends than if you were thinking of doing the same exciting thing on your own. Risk-taking with friends really seems as though it might be more exciting. (If you're interested in reading more about this, there are some references in Resources.)

Why am I telling you this? Because a group mentality can sometimes lead to negative behaviours such as ganging up on someone else. It can lead to people not considering the effects of these behaviours on others because they are having so much fun doing that group thing. Groups often react and behave emotionally, without thinking. The individuals may hardly register that they've hurt anyone by their laughter, exclusion or thoughtless comments. They are just too busy going along with the others. Afterwards, they might feel sorry, but it will be difficult for them to tell you, because that would require one of them to step out of line and say so, risking losing the respect of the others.

Adults behave badly in groups, too. In your school staffroom, I bet there are group behaviours and cliques. I've visited hundreds of staffrooms during my work and I've often noticed the different subject staff sitting separately, in their "territory". Sometimes the librarian or English teacher will tell me, "We can't sit over there, because that's where the maths staff sit." There's no rule that says so: it just is. And you'll get divisions of age or gender and all sorts of other things, too.

Most people are not horrible at heart. We are imperfect, we make mistakes, and we are often too wrapped up in ourselves to behave perfectly towards others. Those negative behaviours become more likely when we're in a group, because we're not acting individually and we can lose a bit of responsibility and self-awareness. It's just easier to forget or not notice what's going on outside the group. Most people would not be unkind on their own, especially face-to-face. Unless, as I've already suggested, they are damaged, ill, stressed, or for some other reason not fully in control of themselves.

THE BYSTANDER EFFECT

This is a well-studied aspect of human behaviour: when something bad is happening, bystanders often do surprisingly little to prevent it. Each of those bystanders may be a good person, but studies indicate that there is a high chance of them not stepping in to help. Some studies appear to show that the more people are present, the less likely one of them is to do something about it, but some researchers have argued against this interpretation. (See Resources.)

There are lots of possible reasons why a good person might not step forward to help someone in need: people can be self-conscious, not confident enough to put themselves in the limelight; they might be thinking, *Someone else will do it* or *Maybe it will resolve itself without my help*; they might think it's a personal situation and they shouldn't interfere, or that they might make it worse; they might be scared, if the situation looks violent. They might think, *Well, no one else is doing anything so it can't really be an emergency*. As stepping in to help is difficult and might be dangerous or frightening, part of our mind is occupied with keeping ourselves safe, so we find all sorts of reasons not to get involved. Often people walk away and then think, *I wish I'd stepped in. Why didn't I?*

173

If the bad behaviour is being done by a group and you're a bystander, it's even harder to intervene, because it could well be dangerous. I'm not recommending that you intervene if there is any danger, but there are two things you might be able to do. First you could get help from a relevant adult and, if you feel someone is being hurt or about to be hurt, this is the right thing to do if you can. And you might try to show support to the victim by giving them a sympathetic look or a few words of understanding later. You might ask them if there's anything they would like you to do. You have the right to keep yourself safe, but there could well be something you can do afterwards to help that person.

SOCIAL MEDIA AND GROUP BEHAVIOUR

Social media can make group behaviour worse because you're not able to see the face and reactions of the person you've hurt. This is the "online disinhibition effect" I mentioned in Section One, which describes how people find themselves behaving online in a way they just wouldn't do face-to-face. There have been too many tragic stories of people – particularly teenagers – being driven to depression, self-harm and even suicide after receiving streams of ugly, cruel and vicious comments over social media. The bullies can quickly gang up and start hassling or abusing someone online, and it just feels so easy. If someone else has already started being mean, it's not hard for someone else to copy. And if a particular group has decided to get their kicks out of being foul to a person, then each time one of them says something nasty they get extra status in the group. And all without being able to see how they've hurt someone.

Group or pack behaviour on social media causes problems for adults, too, as people of any age can behave badly, be cruel and have poor self-control. But it can be harder for teenagers in general, because of your brain changes and also huge social pressures and stresses that surround you. So, although lots of teenagers handle social media and group behaviour brilliantly – and often better than adults – many find it harder to have good empathy, control their actions and think carefully enough about their instant responses.

Remember, though, that social media can be a place for good groups as well as bad ones. Having a place where you and your friends can chat positively online and support each other is something to be welcomed, not just to talk through any concerns you have but also as a way to get to know a wider range of people. Being part of a positive group online is also low-maintenance, as it doesn't matter if you aren't there every day or don't respond to every comment .

THINGS TO THINK ABOUT
- Anyone who wants to stand up against group

behaviour has to be very strong, because the pressures can be huge. Sometimes you won't manage it, but don't beat yourself up if that happens. (If you can find someone to talk to about the situation, do.) However, think how proud you will feel if you do refuse to go along with something that's wrong. You may get a few mean comments but you will know you did the right thing, and that is a very empowering feeling.

- If you think a group – whether you're in it or not – is behaving cruelly to someone else, don't join in. Try to find a way to walk away, without putting yourself in danger. Although it's difficult to stand up against a group you're part of, it's worse to know you've bullied someone. If this has already happened, think about whether the group is really one you still want to be involved in. Isn't it better to feel good about yourself, even if it means losing so-called friends? There are other, better friends out there and you will find them.

- If you're enjoying being part of a group, whether online or face-to-face, check that you're not accidentally excluding someone. I'm not saying you have a duty to let everyone into your group – of course you don't. But it's possible that, completely without intending to, you are ignoring someone who would love to join you and who will thrive in your group. Making them welcome would help you and them.

- Try to remind yourself that whatever annoying or upsetting situation you find yourself in will soon disappear. The group will change as other influences take over. Just try to rise above any trouble and avoid being the one making things unnecessarily difficult.

- If you are being bullied, or if any group behaviour is making your life a misery, talk to a trusted adult about it. You don't have to name names if you don't want to, but you can still describe a situation and ask for strategies. You'll find some information about bullying in Resources.

How stress and anxiety affect behaviour

Stress and anxiety are part of a natural, positive biological process, which all animals experience. It is designed to be life-saving and performance-enhancing. Supposing something happens that suddenly requires your brain or body to perform super well. For example, there's someone running towards you who looks frightening. Or you see a huge tree falling into your path. In those circumstances, the stress chemicals adrenalin and cortisol rush incredibly quickly through your body. These chemicals make your heart beat faster, sending blood (with oxygen and glucose) to your muscles and brain, where it's needed. This means that you focus brilliantly on the problem and run faster and are stronger than normal. It's sometimes called the "flight, fight or freeze" response, because it allows an animal to either fight hard, run fast, or freeze so still that it can't be seen – whichever gives it the best chance of survival. It is why when we're under pressure – scared or desperate – we can perform super-human feats.

Once you have time to think about how you feel, you'll notice that you feel panicky, nervous, jittery. Your heart is racing, your mouth is dry and your skin is cold. Those are the effects of the stress chemicals, which kick in every time there's something to be nervous about. So, not just emergency situations, such as potential criminals

178

and other extreme physical dangers, but also things like having to stand up in front of an audience and perform, or an exam, football match or interview.

The problem is that, as well as those obvious situations requiring "super performance", our lives are full of very small things that also cause a stress reaction. Things like worrying we're going to be late for something, losing our phone or key, realizing we haven't done our homework, not being able to understand something in class, a person saying something mean – any negative thought, upset or worry, however small. All of them are tiny threats or challenges to our system, and they all produce the chemicals that make us feel a tiny bit (or sometimes very) stressed.

Feeling stressed can make people behave badly. I mentioned this briefly in the chapter "Other People's Lives", suggesting that you need to think about what might be going on in someone's life that could explain their bad behaviour.

It's important to add that one of the stress chemicals, cortisol, has a habit of building up in the body and can have longer-term effects, such as poor sleep, loss of concentration, low mood, weaker immune system, and a general feeling of unwellness.

Someone who is under stress for any reason, or who is suffering those longer-term effects of cortisol build-up, tends to have difficulty controlling their words and actions,

179

and behaving well. This applies equally to adults, by the way, but I think teenagers have more of an excuse, partly because your prefrontal cortex isn't fully developed (the bit that helps you have self-control and empathy); partly because you have so many pressures on you; and partly because you have less *experience* of dealing with stress.

I'M THE ONE WHO'S STRESSED – WHY SHOULD I CARE ABOUT *THEIR* STRESS?

Problems with friendships or peer groups are almost certainly going to be a major cause of stress for you. It's probably partly why you're reading this book. Understanding the minds of the people around you is one thing, but how can you deal with the stress that all this is causing you?

So, let's focus on you. If you're suffering from stress, you could have any (or all) of these: physical symptoms such as headaches and stomach aches; negative thought patterns that won't leave you alone; difficulty sleeping; loss of appetite; difficulty concentrating in class. You may also be feeling very self-critical, thinking you're useless or that your life is going to be bad for ever. And you may be irritable, snapping at friends and family.

You'll be glad to know that, although this doesn't feel very nice, not only is it normal at any age but also there are lots of things you can do which will help. And they are things you should do, as part of looking after yourself.

180

Everything will benefit: your friendships, your wellbeing, and how well you function at school and outside school. You'll find some helpful information in Resources.

THINGS TO THINK ABOUT

- Stress will affect relationships because it affects people's mood and control. When people are stressed, they say things they don't mean and may not have headspace to be such a good friend to you. Don't take this personally.

- When you're stressed, you will also find it harder to be tactful and kind. Don't be hard on yourself if you've said something you regret. If you can, find a way to say sorry. You'll feel a whole load better and so will the other person.

- Whether you're dealing with your own stress or the stressed behaviour of other people, don't forget that talking to a trusted adult can help. This might be in practical ways; or if you can get them to understand how you feel, that alone can be enough to make you feel a bit better. If you think the adults in your household are too stressed to help, then turn to a teacher or someone else you trust. Teachers are a good starting point, as they are less emotionally connected to you and may have a calmer outlook.

- Relaxing is not a luxury; it's not something you should only do when you've finished your work, as a reward. Getting enough relaxation by building "time out" into every day is as important as having the right food, and enough sleep and exercise. All four of those things are necessary for good physical and mental health.

- Learning a good breathing skill is important, too, as this gives you a tool to use when you feel very stressed. Sometimes this is called "belly breathing", because it gets you to focus your breathing low down, below your ribcage, rather than high up in your chest.

QUIZ

Is stress affecting your behaviour?

Unless you are made of steel and stronger than most adults, stress will almost certainly affect your behaviour. But sometimes people don't realize how stressed they are: they may be so used to the feelings or symptoms that they don't recognize them as stress-related. This quiz will give you some insight into that.

Remember that stress varies from day to day and month to month, but what's important for this is *now*, so your answers should relate to how you feel at the moment or have felt during the last couple of weeks.

Give yourself a score of 0, 1, 2, 3 or 4, depending on how strongly you agree with the following statements: 0 for "not at all", 4 for "extremely".

1. Most days I have a headache or stomach ache without an obvious cause. (Obvious causes might be when you have a cold or other virus, when you've eaten something bad or you have period pains, for example.)
2. I often miss what a teacher or other adult says because I'm worrying about something, so I have difficulty concentrating.

3. I am snappy and irritable a lot of the time. People annoy me more than usual.

4. I'm not sleeping well. I take a long time to get to sleep or if I wake up, I lie there worrying.

5. I often feel nervous without knowing why.

6. I have lost my appetite, although I quite often want to eat sweet things and snack. Sometimes I can't tell if I feel sick or hungry.

7. Sometimes I feel I can't get a full breath into my lungs, as though I am trying to sigh but I can't. It's as if a weight is crushing my chest.

8. I quite often feel dizzy.

9. There's something going on in my life which is occupying most of my thoughts.

10. When I think about my future, I feel anxious and scared, more than excited.

11. The only way I seem to finish work is to get up early or work late at night.

12. I never, or almost never, do something deliberately for relaxation.

13. I often feel quite panicky when I think of everything I have to do, and this makes it hard to know where to start.

14. Often when I'm studying, I find I'm reading a passage over and over but not taking any of it in.

15. I'm very clumsy just now. I've dropped or broken something or bumped into furniture more than once in the last couple of days.

If you scored more than 40 out of 60, think about the following: first, is there something, such as an exam or a performance, that is making you particularly anxious? If so, focus on the fact that this will soon be over and you will feel better. Then look at the pattern of your scores: if you scored 3 or 4 on lots of things but 0–2 on the others, it may help you to think of small changes which could make a difference. For example, you could set aside time to relax each day and weekend; or you could learn a breathing skill to use if you feel dizzy. (You'll find information in Resources.)

Whatever the cause of your high score, you will feel and perform much better if you can practise some simple relaxation and anti-stress techniques.

And Finally...

Friendships are amazingly varied. How or why they work and don't work can be hard to pin down and sometimes impossible to do so. But they matter. They matter to how we feel about ourselves and how we feel about life. They matter to our health and wellbeing. The knowledge that you have someone to turn to, who wants to share some time, some laughter, some thoughts with you, who knows stuff about you, who cares – all that makes an incredible difference. When that's going right, you feel you can get on with the other parts of your life. In fact, when friendships are going right, we don't always think about them. We might take them for granted.

Perhaps you're reading this book because your friendships haven't been going quite right. You may even have got it into your head that you're too shy, too boring, too different, too something, and you'll never be the most "popular" girl or boy in the class. You were probably blaming yourself, wondering what you could or should do to change things. I hope I've shown you that you shouldn't blame yourself, and that if people treat you badly it's their fault, not yours. But I hope I've also shown you how to look at other people's behaviour and your own. Because sometimes there are things we can do to help people realize who we are, to show them that there is more to everyone than meets the eye, and to make them value good friendship and all the support it brings.

There are three points I want to end with.

First, I think the teenage years are very often the worst stage of your life for all this stuff. Being a teenager can be exciting and you don't have the burden of paying bills and rent, but you are also in a crowded hothouse of far too many people with stormy emotions, constant change and expectations of perfection. You feel everyone's watching you. It's often tough. And it can be worse than tough for some people: it can seem overwhelming.

That links to my second point. I've said this before but it's so important that it is worth repeating: remember that everything changes and where we are now is just a phase. Adults can be very annoying when they say adolescence is "just a phase" but that's not what I'm saying: I'm saying *everything* is a phase. Everything in the world is in a constant state of "flux", or change, including the cells in your body, the connections in your brain, every thought, desire, ability, wish, ambition, dream: it's all changing, bit by bit. And some of that change you will be able to control, bit by bit.

My third and final point is: you'll forget. You'll forget how you feel now – almost all of it, perhaps even *all* of it. Humans have a very healthy tendency to amnesia; we forget an enormous amount of what happens to us. We sometimes forget it entirely, but even if we remember that a particular thing happened, we always forget exactly

187

how bad it felt. It's like the sensations of hot or cold: when you're too hot, you can't conjure up the memory of exactly what it's like to be too cold, and vice versa.

I have forgotten every single one of the arguments, break-ups and bad times I had with friends at school. Every. Single. One. I know there must have been some. I have a vague memory of having two friends who didn't like each other, which caused some problems for me – and presumably for them. But I don't remember the feelings. I told you that I remember being left out of things in my peer group, though I don't recall feeling sad. I must have done, but if I can't remember, it's no big deal, is it? And this is my point: it must have been a big deal at the time, but it vanished into the mists of my memory.

Thank goodness for amnesia, eh?

The good things you have now will last as long as they're designed to last and the bad times will last as long as you allow them to. Be strong, ride out the negatives and embrace the positives; widen your net, be open to new experiences, new people to support you and to support, new understanding and new friends, some of whom will grow and change with you to become the old friends of your future. You don't know which they will be but you will be there for each other because that's what good friends are for.

Resources

Throughout this book, I've referred to topics you might like to investigate further. I've included some references here, as well as a few general sources of support or interest. Although I'm based in the UK, the materials I've listed are from a variety of countries. If the research is strong, it doesn't make any difference where in the world it comes from, but it's also worth remembering that your country will have its own organisations and websites which you might find suit you better, and it wouldn't be possible for me to list sites from everywhere. The ones I've provided will give you a start.

I hope you'll want to research more widely yourself by using a library or the Internet. If you're using the Internet, remember that there is some very poor-quality "information" out there and we all have to be careful to judge what is valid and what isn't. Make sure that what you read is written by people who genuinely know their subject and are not just trying to sell you something or making an opinion look like well-researched fact. Also, if you are using newspapers and magazines, whether online or print, remember that the journalists often simply don't have time to delve into the facts behind the research or the space to give the details.

When you do an Internet search, I recommend you begin by focusing on large organisations such as universities or governments; major medical organisations – for example, the NHS in the UK or the National Institute of Mental Health (NIMH) in the US; recognized charities or large, well-funded websites – for example, YoungMinds or Psych Central; and well-known journals – for example, *Scientific American Mind* or *Psychology Today*. Look at charities, groups and organisations that focus on whichever topic you want and try to assess whether the materials are written by experts. Many of these searches will then lead you to local support networks and smaller groups which can also be extremely helpful. There are also online articles, forums, blogs and websites dedicated to a particular topic and many of these can be really useful.

Importantly, I recommend you don't just listen to or read one person's or even one organisation's view. If you find that several major sites or resources are saying the same thing, it's much more likely that they are offering quality information. Lots of people saying something doesn't prove it's true but it's a good start. It's important to question and disagree sometimes, of course, but anyone who questions or disagrees with what other experts are saying needs to have a strong argument and evidence.

So, don't just believe the first thing you read and definitely don't just believe the headline: headlines can be very misleading.

NB Where I have mentioned the universities where certain academics work, I have named the university where they were when they did the research in question. They may now be working at different organisations.

General support and information

CHILDLINE

Childline is a hugely respected UK charity that enables young people to speak to a trained adult safely and confidentially about whatever worries they have. Childline has a "confidentiality promise" on its website, explaining that what you say to their counsellors stays between you and them but there are occasions when they may need to get you emergency help. You can also chat to them online. As well as the opportunities to contact them, you will also find lots of advice on the site. Remember that when you visit any site, including Childline, it can show up in your computer or phone's browsing history. If you want to avoid this, take steps to clear your history. Visit their website: **www.childline.org.uk/** Or you can call them free (in the UK) on 0800 1111.

YOUNGMINDS

YoungMinds is another well-respected UK charity working to improve young people's wellbeing and mental health and to break down ignorance and stigma surrounding mental illness of all sorts. The website has advice, support and well-researched information on a range of issues affecting young people: **www.youngminds.org.uk/**

Specific Issues

ANXIETY

If you are suffering from anxieties or fears that are spoiling your ability to function and affecting your wellbeing, YoungMinds has an excellent section: **www.youngminds.org. uk/for_children_young_people/whats_worrying_you/anxiety/** Do remember that feeling anxious or afraid is entirely normal and healthy but it is easy to feel overwhelmed by these feelings or to experience them more than is healthy. If you think that applies to you, don't suffer in silence. Click on the "Anxiety help" section of the YoungMinds site.

A useful book is *The Anxiety Workbook for Teens: Activities to Help You Deal with Anxiety and Worry* by Lisa M. Schab.

And one for teenagers to build positive feelings about themselves is *Banish Your Self-Esteem Thief,* by Kate Collins-Donnelly.

(See also Neuroticism and Social Anxiety Disorder)

BULLYING AND CYBER-BULLYING

Bullying UK is an important site, tackling and advising on many separate aspects of bullying in a friendly and accessible way: **www.bullying.co.uk/**

Beyond Bullying also has a range of articles on different aspects of bullying, and includes explanations and strategies, as well as helpful resources: **www.beyondbullying.com/**

Kidscape is a charity working to give adults and young people the skills to prevent and tackle bullying. In their resources section, there is a PDF called "Cyber-bullying: Advice for young people", offering advice for young people on bullying, cyber-bullying and online safety: **www.kidscape.org.uk/**

BYSTANDER EFFECT

There's a clear introduction to the Bystander Effect in *Psychology Today*: **www.psychologytoday.com/basics/bystander-effect/** You'll see that the phrase started after the murder of Kitty Genovese in 1964, witnessed by several people who didn't intervene; it was their lack of intervention that prompted a lot of research over later years into whether and why groups seem less likely to intervene to prevent abuse or aggression than individuals. In that introduction, you'll find links to various articles, including one by Dr Melissa Burkley, which delves more deeply into the subject. ("Why Don't We Help? Less Is More, at Least When it Comes to Bystanders.")

Dr Philip Zimbardo is a world expert in the bystander effect and the US website Bystander Revolution has a video of him explaining it. The direct link to his video is here: **www.bystanderrevolution.org/v/Dr.+Philip+Zimbardo+%7C+The+Bystander+Effect/wW2xszD-zBM/**

If you go to the Bystander Effect page of the Bystander Revolution website, you will see many other videos but more importantly you will also find sections for "Problems" and "Solutions", all divided into categories so you can easily find the ones that are relevant to you: **www.bystanderrevolution.org/browse/bystandereffect/**

EMPATHY

Male/female differences – This is a controversial topic and I recommend you read a range of opinions to get a balanced view. But there's no doubt you'll find more research showing that, on average, females have greater empathy skills than research showing no difference, or showing that males have more empathy. (If this is true, we still don't know how much this difference is caused by something we are born with and how much by the way boys and girls are brought up and how they are moulded by society, though many people have strong views on both sides.) Focus on studies done by major universities and using large numbers of people and/or spanning many years. For example, a 2009 study into adolescents – "Are women more empathetic than men? A longitudinal study in adolescence" by Mestre, Samper and others, published in *The Spanish Journal of Psychology* – reported "a greater empathic response in females than in males of the same age, differences growing with age".

Professor Simon Baron-Cohen, Professor of Developmental Psychopathology at the University of Cambridge, has researched into empathy (as part of work on aspects of autism) and his findings are covered in his book, *The Essential Difference: Men, Women and the Extreme Male Brain*.

For a different perspective, try *Delusions of Gender: The Real Science Behind Sex Differences*, by academic psychologist and writer, Cordelia Fine. She argues, with supporting research, that any differences in empathetic response are not biological but created by the environment and society we grow up in.

Empathy and reading/stories – My own website has a

section where I have gathered resources on what reading does in the brain, including the effects on empathy: **www.nicolamorgan.com/category/reading-brain-readaxation/** In the post called "Big News About #Readingforpleasure" you will find a discussion about a major review carried out by The Reading Agency in 2015 in which they assessed hundreds of pieces of research – "Literature Review: the impact of reading for pleasure and empowerment". You can read that review in full here: **https://readingagency.org.uk/news/media/reading-for-pleasure-builds-empathy-and-improves-wellbeing-research-from-the-reading-agency-finds.html**

EmpathyLab – This small but exciting organisation works in schools to educate about the links between reading and empathy. Ask your school librarian or teacher about getting in touch and creating an empathy project in your school: **www.empathylab.uk/**

(See also Teenage Brain Development)

GENDER AND SEXUALITY

Stonewall is a UK organisation campaigning for "acceptance without exception" for lesbian, gay, bi-sexual and trans people. It has a special section called Young Stonewall, for young people who are lesbian, gay, bi, trans or questioning their gender and/or sexuality, so that they "can live their lives free from discrimination and fulfil their potential". The home page is: **www.youngstonewall.org.uk?/** There you will see a section called "LGBTQ info", which has subsections on Sexual Orientation and Gender Identity. Young Stonewall offers excellent information and support, whatever your situation. It's an important site for everyone to look at, whether or not they are personally affected by the issues raised, because it helps improve understanding by all.

The author for Young Adults, Juno Dawson, has written a popular book, *This Book is Gay*. Your school librarian will be able to suggest other books – both fiction and non-fiction – that might interest and help you.

INTROVERSION AND EXTROVERSION

The Quiet Revolution website and the work of Susan Cain are ideal starting points: **www.quietrev.com/**

Cain's latest book, published in 2016, is *Quiet Power: The Secret Strengths of Introverts*, and is specifically aimed at teenagers, schools and parents. It's a reworking of her popular book published in 2012, *Quiet: The Power of Introverts in a World that Can't Stop Talking*. Of course, these books are about introversion but they also reveal insights into extroversion. Some people find them biased in favour of introverts, putting too much weight on the value of introverts above extroverts. That's a fair point, but Cain is trying to defend introverts in a world where she sees them as often being undervalued. I recommend *Quiet Power* to all teachers, as I think it's important that everyone working with young people understands how they may be feeling in classroom and other school situations, but I also think it's an important subject for anyone.

You might also like an article on Psych Central, which offers a

more balanced view of introversion/extroversion:
www.psychcentral.com/blog/archives/2013/09/11/7-persistent-myths-about-introverts-extroverts/

KINDNESS TO OTHERS

Many studies show that kindness benefits the giver as well as the receiver. The Authentic Happiness website is a good place to start: **www.authentichappiness.sas.upenn.edu/** Or try this article in *Psychology Today*: **www.psychologytoday.com/blog/the-social-self/201012/giving-really-is-better-receiving/**

Random Acts of Kindness is a project you might be interested in, with lots of ideas for doing small things to help you and others: **www.randomactsofkindness.org/**

LUNCH-TIME CHALLENGES – WHO TO SIT WITH?

I can't imagine there's anyone who doesn't understand that entering a dining-hall and not having someone to sit with is a really unpleasant experience. We all go through it when we are new somewhere but sometimes other people can make it truly horrible by either not noticing that we are alone or by deliberately excluding us. So, you'll be glad to know that there is help.

The app, SitWithUs, was created by 16-year-old Natalie Hampton after her own negative experiences of lunchtime behaviour: **http://sitwithus.io./#!/Home** You need a number of people at your school to have the app but this is something I think your school or class teacher could quite easily introduce.

Beyond Differences is a US organisation committed to

ending social isolation and it has a range of inspiring activities and ideas: **www.beyonddifferences.org/** One of its projects is No One Eats Alone, which was created and led by students: **www.nooneeatsalone.org/** There is an annual #NoOneEatsAloneDay, which is a good focus of attention but, of course, every day should be a No One Eats Alone Day. There is a free resource pack for US schools, but it shouldn't be difficult for a school anywhere in the world to create its own project based around the concept. All that is required is for students to commit to making sure that no one has to sit alone at lunch! You could have badges that students might wear to show that they are involved, for example. It's not hard to do once you think about it and it will make everyone feel better, not just the people who would otherwise have been alone.

You might consider using the World Kindness Day concept to launch your school's campaign: **www.kindnessuk.com/world_kindness_day_kindness_day_uk.php** And it would work very well as a "random act of kindness" – see KINDNESS TO OTHERS, the previous item in these resources.

MACHIAVELLIAN BEHAVIOUR

I mentioned research suggesting that many people will act cruelly in certain circumstances – more people than would actually consider themselves cruel. Two of the best-known studies into variations of this are the Milgram Experiment of 1963, which got people to administer what they mistakenly thought were electric shocks to a stranger who was in fact acting a part; and the Stanford Prison Experiment of 1971, which gave people prisoner or guard roles and observed the levels of cruelty that ordinary people would reach when they were "following rules". An Internet search for either of these will quickly take you to various discussions about what the research may reveal and the follow-up research that has been done. If you choose to study psychology at school or college, you will certainly spend time discussing these experiments, as so much has been written about them.

NARCISSISM

There is a good introduction to this personality trait on the *Psychology Today* website: **www.psychologytoday.com/basics/narcissism**

Note that narcissism is not itself a personality disorder so make sure you don't confuse "often thinking of oneself" or "having high self-esteem" with a narcissistic personality disorder. To see what I mean, I recommend you read this article, "Self-esteem versus narcissism" by Dr Lisa Firestone: **www.psychologytoday.com/blog/compassion-matters/201206/self-esteem-versus-narcissism**

NEUROTICISM

Again, *Psychology Today* is a good place to start understanding neuroticism: **www.psychologytoday.com/basics/neuroticism/** You'll find more articles linked on that page.

(See also Anxiety and Social Anxiety Disorder. Anxiety is an aspect of neuroticism but anxiety is also a healthy natural response to the things around us.)

PERSONALITY TESTS

There are many free online personality or psychological profiling tests, some of which are better than others. The free ones tend to provide a basic interpretation and you would have to pay for a more detailed report. I don't recommend that you pay for one of these online tests, as it's difficult to know which are worthwhile and you could be wasting your money. Trained psychologists carry out expert tests and, of course, those are not free but they are much more likely to reveal "true" things about your personality and to give greater detail.

Remember that, as with the quizzes in this book, online tests can only give you a basic snapshot of an aspect of your personality at this particular time and do not define who you are or who you might become. They give you clues and may provide insight but you shouldn't attach more to them than that.

A good starting point for free online tests is *Psychology Today*: **psychologytoday.tests.psychtests.com/**
Another useful site, where you can test your "24 character strengths", is the VIA Institute on Character: **www.viacharacter.org/www/** At the time of writing, the introductory quiz for this was free but you have to register. Do check with an adult in case you are required to give personal information. I know many schools use the materials.

SOCIAL ANXIETY AND SOCIAL ANXIETY DISORDER

Social Anxiety Disorder (SAD), and the less severe form, Social Anxiety (SA), cause sufferers to avoid many or all social or performance situations because of extreme anxiety. It is often associated with school phobia or school refusal. You'll also hear it called Social Phobia. "Phobia" is the Greek word for "fear" but note that a true phobia involves a really extreme reaction to something, with a racing heart and feelings of panic which stop the person being able to act or think rationally.

You can find out more about it on this US site: **http://teenmentalhealth.org/learn/mental-disorders/social-anxiety-disorder/**

A good UK site is: **www.social-anxiety.org.uk/**

There is a brief screening test here: **http://psymed.info/social-anxiety-test/** Note that this on its own does not prove whether you have the disorder, which should be diagnosed by an expert. But, if you are worried by your results, talk to an adult you trust and/or see your doctor for further help. The condition is not likely to go away by itself but can improve greatly with professional support. You can be taught many strategies to help you manage situations that you find difficult and reduce your anxiety levels, so it's definitely worth getting help and not suffering in silence.

The usual medical treatment for SAD is Cognitive Behavioural Therapy (CBT), which is a very well-known and often highly effective "talking therapy" and works by altering your thought patterns so that you become less anxious and have healthier mental processes. Standard relaxation and stress-relief strategies will also be helpful for managing symptoms, and learning a relaxed breathing technique will be very useful to carry you through times when you feel anxious.

(You will find some mentioned under stress management and relaxation.)

Social Anxiety Support (a US organisation) has a forum for teenagers: **www.socialanxietysupport.com/forum/f49/** But it's important to get proper help first, to have a diagnosis and a better understanding of how the condition applies to you, and to follow expert advice that is tailored to you.

SOCIAL CREATURES

Robin Dunbar is Professor of Evolutionary Psychology at the University of Oxford and his work investigates how certain mammals, including humans, make social bonds and what those bonds are for. His book, *Grooming, Gossip and the Evolution of Language*, argues that humans evolved language as part of the bonding process, and includes an explanation of his theory known as "Dunbar's Number", which suggests that 150 is the number of relationships an average human can maintain – a number that is far larger than any other animal and almost three times as big as the social groups of the chimpanzee, our nearest relative. Dunbar suggests that human gossip has the same social purpose as the grooming behaviour of other primates when they pick fleas out of each other's fur! There is a good introduction to these ideas here: **www.humanjourney.us/thinkingBig.html**

SOCIAL MEDIA

Beyond Bullying has an excellent set of resources on how to be safe on social media. It includes survey facts as well as safety tips and advice: **www.beyondbullying.com/cyberbullying.html/**

Childline also has an excellent section on online safety: **https://childline.org.uk/info-advice/bullying-abuse-safety/online-mobile-safety/staying-safe-online/**

Does using the Internet and social media change your brain? Well, yes, because everything we do changes our brain in some way and the more time we spend on a particular activity, the more changes there will be in whatever brain areas that activity uses. It is obviously too early for research into long-term effects yet, but it is something scientists are starting to look at properly and there are some early results. As a starting point, check out this excellent fifteen-minute talk, "The effect of internet use and networking culture on the adolescent brain (2013)" by researcher Kate Mills: **https://sites.google.com/site/blakemorelab/talks/katemills89plus** (The first five minutes are about the teenage brain in general but it soon focuses on social networking behaviour. Be warned, though: it's quite technical!)

STRESS MANAGEMENT AND RELAXATION

My book, *The Teenage Guide to Stress*, covers many things that I think you'll find helpful and there are lots of free resources on my website at **www.nicolamorgan.com**, including an audio of a relaxation/breathing exercise, which you can download. My philosophy is that it's incredibly beneficial and empowering when we understand how stress works in our bodies and how it brings benefits as well as possible problems. My website and books offer this understanding, as well as many simple strategies you can use throughout your life.

For other breathing exercises, do an Internet search for "belly-breathing" or "4-7-8 breathing".

There are apps such as Headspace and MindShift (both are free or partly free and available for Apple iOS and Android devices). Or you can download relaxing music on to your phone. You'll find other free apps offering meditation or mindfulness tools. Mindfulness is a form of meditation, encouraging you to focus on your breathing and other things inside you or around you, to try to centre your thinking and calm it down when negative thoughts are side-tracking your attention.

My website also has resources on using reading for pleasure as a stress management tool: **www.nicolamorgan.com/category/reading-brain-readaxation/** "Readaxation" is a word I invented and it means, "The deliberate act of reading to relax, improving wellbeing and performance." It's almost the same as "reading for pleasure" – and certainly pleasure is a big part of it, but readaxation describes what the science now tells us about the stress-relieving benefits of reading something that you enjoy. You'll find the research referenced in that section of my site.

A very useful workbook with practical ways of relaxing and reducing stress is *The Stress Reduction Workbook for Teens: Mindfulness skills to help you deal with stress* by Gina M. Biegel.

And another book that could be helpful is *Fighting Invisible Tigers* by Earl Hipp.

TEENAGE BRAIN DEVELOPMENT

General – My book, *Blame My Brain – The Amazing Teenage Brain Revealed*, explains adolescent changes in emotions, sleep, risk-taking, depression/mental illness, male/female brains and an increase in thinking skills.

Professor Sarah-Jayne Blakemore is Professor of Cognitive Neuroscience at University College London and is well-known for her research into many aspects of adolescence. She and her team have looked at the brains of many teenagers inside "functional Magnetic Resonance Imaging" (fMRI) scanners, machines that can see which brain areas are working during different mental activities. Blakemore has a talk here: **www.ted.com/talks/sarah_jayne_blakemore_the_mysterious_ workings_of_the_adolescent_brain/**

Risk-taking – There's masses of research into this and different angles you might want to consider. My advice is to do an Internet search for "adolescent risk-taking" and then focus on results reported by any of the major organisations I mentioned in the introduction to this Resources section.

Social embarrassment – Some of the most focused research into this is done by Professor Sarah-Jayne Blakemore and colleagues at UCL. Some of her team's research into this is available on her website, **Blakemore Lab: https://sites.google. com/site/blakemorelab/research/**

Empathy – I mentioned that teenagers in general, and particularly younger ones, may have more difficulty with empathy than older age groups. (Remember that this is based on averages and that there will be many teenagers with excellent empathy and many adults with poor empathy.) I also mentioned research showing that younger teenagers tend to be less good than others at recognizing what someone might be feeling based on their facial expression or eyes. To follow this up, look for work by Dr Deborah Yurgelun-Todd, Professor of Psychiatry at the University of Utah. Here is an interview in which she talks about her research into the teenage brain and empathy: **www.pbs.org/wgbh/pages/frontline/shows/teenbrain/interviews/todd.html**

This article in *The Wall Street Journal* includes references to a number of research scientists working in this area, including Professor Sarah-Jayne Blakemore: **www.wsj.com/articles/SB10001424052702304561004579137514122387446/**
On that page, you'll find a video interview with two authors who have written books about this: **www.wsj.com/video/why-do-teens-only-think-about-themselves/1DC71669-E7A1-497D-A92F-0CD2F14310E4.html**

I must add that I find it depressing how negative the reporting about teenage empathy often is. Considering that newspaper articles are written by adults, I frankly don't think many of them show empathy themselves! The references I've cited and the work of the scientists themselves do show empathy, but much of the media reporting of the research seems to lack that understanding.

THEORY OF MIND

Theory of Mind (usually abbreviated to ToM) is about the ability to understand that what is in your mind may not be what is in another person's mind, and to be able to guess something about what another person knows, thinks, feels or intends. It allows us to predict what other people will do or say, based on what we can work out about their state of mind. Without this ability, it is hard to communicate effectively because good communication relies on knowing something of what the other person knows or wants to know.

The scientists who coined this term in 1978, David Premack and Guy Woodruff, suggested that other primates such as chimpanzees probably have a degree of ToM but at a simpler level than humans. Human infants don't have ToM but it develops from around the age of four and continues to develop throughout adolescence. You can find a clear explanation of Theory of Mind on the *Psychology Today* website: **www.psychologytoday.com/blog/aspergers-diary/200805/empathy-mindblindness-and-theory-mind/** And there's a wonderful video on YouTube showing a researcher explaining and demonstrating the tests with some young children: **www.youtube.com/watch?v=YGSj2zY2OEM/**

Index

Enjoyed *The Teenage Guide to Friends*?
We'd love to hear your thoughts!

🐦 @nicolamorgan
@WalkerBooksUK @WalkerBooksYA

📷 @WalkerBooksYA

And for information about Nicola's books and events,
visit her website: **www.nicolamorgan.com**

NICOLA MORGAN

The Teenage Guide to

STRESS

INCLUDES

exams • relationships • social media & cyber-bullying
depression • eating disorders • drugs & alcohol

The Teenage Guide to Stress

Winner of the School Library Association Award 2015, with both the judges' and readers' awards

Being a teenager can be incredibly stressful. The pressure of exams, changing bodies, social media, bullying and relationships can lead to low self-esteem, depression, anxiety and ill health. *The Teenage Guide to Stress* examines all these problems and more, with great strategies for beating them.

This detailed and sympathetic book reassures teenagers – and the adults who care about them – that they are not alone. And that they CAN beat stress.

- **Looks at the specific worries and fears of teenagers**
- **Suggests positive strategies for healthy minds and bodies**
- **Includes websites and resources**

"A fantastic self-help book... Just the process of reading this book is cathartic but the guidance provided is wonderful." *Guardian*

"I've read many books on the subject of stress, but for me, this one was the most useful ... she has certainly made me feel as though I'm not alone, and that I can deal with stress, even if it seems like I can't." *Guardian Children's Book Website*

"Essential reading for teenagers and the adults who care about them" *Bookseller Children's Guide*

NICOLA MORGAN

BLAME MY BRAIN

NEW
UPDATED
EDITION

THE
AMAZING
TEENAGE
BRAIN
REVEALED

Blame My Brain

Shortlisted for the Aventis prize for science-writing

Scientific research shows what parents have long suspected – the teenage brain IS special! Find out how in this ground-breaking, reassuring and hugely enjoyable book.

From taking risks to sleeping late and depression, uncontrollable emotions to the effects of drugs and alcohol, *Blame My Brain* tells you everything you need to know about the biology and psychology behind the behaviour. Essential reading for teenagers – and parents.

- **Cutting edge science *(that won't make your head spin)***
- **Revealing tests and quizzes**
- **New information on mirror neurons, untidy bedrooms and more!**

"Nicola Morgan has that rare gift of being able to communicate science and make it fun."
Professor Simon Baron-Cohen, University of Cambridge

"This is a good resource to share with students to help them deal with what is potentially the most challenging, but also the most exciting, period in their development."
The Times Educational Supplement

"It's really good and it taught me a lot about my brain ..."
(Ross Rae, 13)

"... and me a lot about my son!" (George Rae, 45)